William E. Studwell *(William Emmett)*, *1936 –*
Bruce R. Schueneman

College Fight Songs II
A Supplementary Anthology

*Pre-publication
REVIEWS,
COMMENTARIES,
EVALUATIONS . . .*

"**A** worthy companion to the previous volume. It is particularly valuable for the historical light it sheds on past fight songs and the evolution of current fight songs at many of our major colleges. As with the previous volume, the inclusion of newly typeset versions of the songs themselves is especially welcome and helpful to scholars."

Timothy E. Scheurer, PhD
*Professor of Humanities,
Franklin University,
Columbus, Ohio*

"**T**he genre specifically known as the 'fight song'—the college march or pep song traditionally played during autumn football games, as well as on other occasions—had received no serious attention in print until Bruce R. Schueneman and William E. Studwell published their anthology *College Fight Songs: An Annotated Anthology* (Haworth Press, 1998). Now the compilers have supplemented their already splendid work with a new volume, structured in the same easy-to-use format as the earlier anthology. The song texts, many of which are in the public domain, are provided with piano accompaniments of a substantially pianistic but readily playable texture, ac-

cessible to amateur pianists and simultaneously capable of appreciation by more advanced players. The inclusion of the musical accompaniments together with the words will permit ready renditions at the piano, whether as material for solo enjoyment or for good old-fashioned sing-alongs. As in the first volume, historical notes have been provided for all songs included in the given volume. Written in a clear, expository style accessible to the general reader, the historical notes constitute a wealth of hard-to-find information on the songs and their origins, providing background on the cultural context from which each song emerged. While in every way as usable as the earlier anthology, the new volume nevertheless contains some important new features. The scope of the supplemental volume surpasses that of the first volume, containing fully ninety-six texts (words and music together) of songs not included earlier. The historical notes contain a substantial amount of new information, together with corrected information based on sources discovered subsequent to the 1998 work. In addition, a list of the twenty-five greatest college fight songs constitutes a ready reference of must-know college fight songs, guiding the reader to the essential standards in this repertory.

Together with the sixty-seven songs contained in the first volume, the ninety-six songs included in the new work account for a total of 163 songs representing ninety-eight colleges and universities in all fifty states. In seeking to fill in the gap in the published literature with a reference work providing not only words and music, but also providing historical background *about* the songs, the compilers may be said to have succeeded admirably. While accessible to the interested general reader, the book's information will also serve reference librarians as a helpful source. Together with its predecessor volume, *College Fight Songs II: A Supplemental Anthology* will be an important addition to the corps of standard reference works on the shelves of public libraries and academic music libraries alike."

David Peter Coppen, MS, CAS

*Special Collections
Librarian and Archivist,
Sibley Music Library,
Eastman School of Music,
Rochester, NY*

College Fight Songs II
A Supplementary Anthology

College Fight Songs II
A Supplementary Anthology

William E. Studwell
Bruce R. Schueneman

The Haworth Press®
New York • London • Oxford

The Haworth Press, Inc., 10 Alice Street, Binghamton, NY 13904-1580

Cover design by Marylouise E. Doyle.

ISBN 0-7890-0920-X—ISBN 0-7890-0921-8 (pbk.).

CONTENTS

ABOUT THE AUTHORS

William E. Studwell, MA, MSLS, is Professor and Principal Cataloger at the University Libraries of Northern Illinois University in DeKalb. The author of *Barbershops, Bullets, and Ballads: An Annotated Anthology of Underappreciated American Musical Jewels, 1865-1918; College Fight Songs: An Annotated Anthology; Publishing Glad Tidings: Essays on Christmas Music;* and *State Songs of the United States: An Annotated Anthology* (The Haworth Press, Inc.), Mr. Studwell is also the author of thirteen other books on music, including reference books on popular songs, national songs, Christmas songs, ballets, and operas. He has written three books on cataloging and almost 340 articles on library science and music. A nationally known expert on carols, college fight songs, and Library of Congress subject headings, he has made approximately 480 radio, television, and print appearances in national, regional, and local media.

Bruce R. Schueneman, MLS, MS, is Head of the Systems Department at Texas A&M University-Kingsville. A violinist, Mr. Schueneman has a special interest in the French Violin School composers. He has published a book and several articles on Pierre Rode, one of the leading French School composers, and has also penned a series of articles on minor composers. Mr. Schueneman has collaborated with William Studwell on several Haworth Press books, including *Minor Ballet Composers* and *State Songs of the United States,* and is currently at work on new editions of scores by Pierre Rode and Cecil Burleigh.

Preface

In 1998, the authors produced *College Fight Songs: An Annotated Anthology* (Binghamton, New York: The Haworth Press). It was a unique volume, publishing sixty-seven song texts and providing brief information on about 200 songs. Although there had been sizable collections of college songs before, no previous volume focused only on fight songs or provided much historical information. In other words, it was by far the most useful publication ever on the subject.

Yet, in spite of commercial success and much attention from various media, it was not as complete as it could have been. Some information that could have been included was not, primarily by design. William Studwell's list of the top twenty-five fight songs, which has appeared in a number of media outlets and in two books (with Studwell's permission) in the last several years, was not included in the 1998 volume. Because it had been widely circulated before, and because its presence in the 1998 volume might be interpreted as suggesting that all songs on the list should be printed in that volume, the list was not included in *College Fight Songs*. In spite of the risk that the inclusion of the list in the present volume might give the reader the impression that it directly correlates with the song texts printed in this volume, the list, updated and amplified, is nevertheless published herein due to extensive interest in it. Most of the songs on the list are printed in either this volume or the 1998 volume. The songs that were not printed were unavailable because permission to publish could not be obtained, despite multiple attempts to acquire them. In addition, what few general comments about the history of American college fight songs that can be formulated are included here, along with a substantial amount of information not found before the completion of the 1998 volume.

Ninety-seven song texts not included in the original volume are printed in this volume, along with matching historical annotations (either new or revised from the original volume). These song texts were not part of the 1998 anthology because of communication problems with the institutions or persons involved, gaps in the authors' knowledge, problems of timing or logistics, or song unavailability for various reasons. Whatever the reason for prior exclusion may have been, we are delighted to be able to present them here. Moreover, in addition to printing a new batch of songs, this supplement offers a substantial amount of new information plus some corrections based on recently discovered sources. (One such correction is the printing of the original version of the famous "The Princeton Cannon Song," which was included in the first volume without words and in a different arrangement.) It is hoped that this work is as well appreciated as was its pioneering predecessor. Collectively, the original volume plus the supplement offer to the public 164 song texts, many not easily available elsewhere, representing ninety-nine colleges and universities, as well as the largest body of historical information yet published. The result is a reasonably comprehensive two-volume coverage, in some depth, of this most interesting but often elusive popular genre.

The authors gratefully acknowledge the kind assistance of the colleges whose songs are printed in this anthology, plus several other institutions who responded to our queries even when circumstances dictated their songs could not be included here. (Unfortunately, some schools chose not to reply, and therefore the missing songs are not necessarily the result of the authors' intent.)

Among the individuals who especially contributed to this enterprise are James D. Pritchard, former director of bands at the University of South Carolina; Francis E. Stroup of DeKalb, Illinois, formerly associated with both the University of North Texas and Northern Illinois University; and Arthur P. Young, Dean, Northern Illinois University Libraries.

A BRIEF HISTORY OF AMERICAN COLLEGE FIGHT SONGS

Without referring to specific songs, little general history exists of American college fight songs. Although students had commonly sung popular ballads, hymns, and excerpts from classical music starting in the eighteenth century, songs specifically composed for institutions of higher learning were not common until the late nineteenth century. The first outstanding song specifically created for college sports was the University of Michigan's "The Victors," written by student Louis Elbel in 1898. It seemed to be a catalyst for similar songs elsewhere, and in the decade following, several exceptional or classic fight songs popped up on American campuses. These include: "Yale Boola" (1901) and "Down the Field" (1904) at Yale University; "The Eyes of Texas" (1903) at the University of Texas at Austin; "The Princeton Cannon Song," also known as "The Cannon Song," (1906) at Princeton University; "The Gridiron King" (1906) at Harvard University; "Anchors Aweigh" (1907) at the United States Naval Academy; and "Notre Dame Victory March" (1908) at the University of Notre Dame.

By World War II most of the better fight songs had been written, and most important academic institutions had at least one lively or endearing piece to serve as a musical symbol of their athletics teams. These pre-World War II songs may seem quaint or innocent when compared to the music of the present era, but together with later similar-style compositions comprise a delightful and culturally significant part of American life. Today very few, if any, colleges or universities are without something energetic to sing or play on public occasions such as intercollegiate competition. In addition, many schools have unofficially adopted various generic or institutionally nonspecific sports songs, most especially a rock arrangement of the old "Hootchy Kootchy Dance," the lively arrangement of which began to be very popular, even ubiquitous, on college campuses starting in the early 1980s. The song was probably written in 1893 for a "Little Egypt" show at the Chicago World's Exposition by Sol Bloom (1870-1949), who was then a press agent and later a congressman from New York State. This type of generic composition seldom if ever replaces the institution-specific fight songs of the schools that use them. Instead, they serve as lively supplements to the other more official pieces.

The term "fight song," coined because of the frequent usage of the word "fight" in titles and/or lyrics, was probably part of everyday collegiate language by the 1940s. Around 1952, a recording by the Lawson-Hoggart Jazz band, on Decca records, actually used the title "College Fight Songs." In recent years, the expression has become familiar to many sectors of our society.

Although usually lively, fight songs have a wide variety of origins. Referring again to early songs, some pieces were completely original, and some pieces were at least partially borrowed. Among the top early songs involved with borrowing are: "The Eyes of Texas," which uses the anonymous 1894 American melody associated with "I've Been Working on the Railroad"; Harvard University's "Our Director," which couples a splendid 1895 melody written by Frederick Ellsworth Bigelow for a purpose not associated with the university with 1912 lyrics specifically geared to the university; and Georgia Institute of Technology's "Rambling Wreck from Georgia Tech," which pairs an anonymous 1873 (or earlier) melody with anonymous 1919 lyrics. Numerous other fight songs have similar derived melodic origins, including the University of Wisconsin at Madison's "On, Wisconsin" (1909), which may well have been influenced by a passage from the first act of Peter Ilich Tchaikovsky's great 1877 ballet *Swan Lake,* and the University of Maine's "The Maine Stein Song" (1910), which is apparently based on a Hungarian dance by Johannes Brahms. Some songs written for one school have been utilized extensively by other schools, for example, the University of Tennessee at Knoxville's loving adoption of Yale University's "Down the Field"; the University of Oklahoma's acquisition of the melody of "Yale Boola" for its sensational "Boomer Sooner"; and the various institutions that have selected the title and/or the melody of Paul P. McNeely's fine "Stand Up and Cheer" (1909), written expressly for the University of Kansas.

Therefore, American college fight songs, although often sounding similar and generally having the same underlying purpose of promoting their institutions through music, are products of a large, complex, and often confusing body of cultural material. To add to this complexity and confusion, one song specifically written as a fight song later became one of the best of American patriotic creations. "Anchors Aweigh" (1907), by Alfred H. Miles and Charles A. Zimmermann, was exclusively the delight of the Naval Academy's midshipmen until 1930, when revised lyrics by George D. Lottman converted it also into "The Song of the Navy." In this new role, it helped lead the United States into much more serious battles in World War II and on other occasions. Therefore, this was one prominent case of a mock fight song becoming a real-life fight song.

The Top Twenty-Five
College Fight Songs

1-10: Great Songs No Matter What the Origins

1. "Notre Dame Victory March" (University of Notre Dame)
   Best known and perhaps the most borrowed
2. "The Victors" (University of Michigan)
   Most rousing and stunning; very proud song
3. "On, Wisconsin" (University of Wisconsin at Madison)
   Smooth and much-borrowed old classic
4. "Down the Field" (Yale University)
   Another smooth and much-borrowed old classic
5. "Anchors Aweigh" (United States Naval Academy)
   Very dynamic and uplifting
6. "The Maine Stein Song" (University of Maine)
   Great melody, but it's a drinking song
7. "Fight on for USC" (University of Southern California)
   Brilliant, sparkling, and innovative
8. "Rambling Wreck from Georgia Tech" (Georgia Institute of Technology)
   Fine tune; great sense of humor; a passing mention to the University of Virginia's "Rugby Road" which also uses the tune
9. "The Eyes of Texas" (University of Texas at Austin)
   Tune borrowed from "I've Been Working on the Railroad," but has a lot of sweep and energy
10. "Across the Field" (Ohio State University)
    Smooth and active; takes one pleasantly across the field

Note: Not all are official fight songs.

11-15: Nearly Great Original Songs

11. "Minnesota Rouser" (University of Minnesota)
    Dynamic and rousing, as the title suggests
12. "Indiana, Our Indiana" (Indiana University)
    Tugs at the heart while causing foot tapping
13. "Illinois Loyalty" (University of Illinois at Urbana-Champaign)
    Smooth, sensitive, and flowing
14. "Washington and Lee Swing" (Washington and Lee University)
    Very catchy and likeable; well-named and often borrowed
15. "Stand Up and Cheer" (University of Kansas)
    Much-borrowed winner worth standing up for (among the schools that have variant songs under the same title are Ohio University and Montana State University)

16-20: Nearly Great but Borrowed Songs

16. "Boomer Sooner" (University of Oklahoma)
    Borrowed from "Yale Boola," but rocks the stadium in Norman when performed by tens of thousands of avid fans; and equal mention to the Yale song which inspired it
17. "Glory, Glory, to Old Georgia" (University of Georgia)
    Uses the rouser "Battle Hymn of the Republic" as its tune; equal mentions to the University of Colorado who also uses the tune for its "Glory, Glory, Colorado" and to Auburn University who uses it for "Glory to Ole Auburn" (the University of Virginia at one time also borrowed the tune for "Glory to Virginia," as did the University of Southern California for "Glory, Southern California" and "USC Is Marching On!" The United States Naval Academy uses the tune for its humorous "The Goat Is Old and Gnarly")
18. "The Air Force Song" (United States Air Force Academy)
    Excellent uplifting march; also used as the Air Force's song
19. "Semper Paratus" (United States Coast Guard Academy)
    Lesser known but quite stirring march; also used as the Coast Guard's song
20. "Fight Song" (Clemson University)
    Uses the delightful "Tiger Rag" as its tune

21-25: Special Category of Definitely Superior Songs Perhaps Selected for Odd Reasons

21. "Down the Field" (University of Tennessee, Knoxville)
    Uses the same title and tune as Yale's great classic "Down the Field," but never is performed with words; F for originality, but A+ for taste; often played from the stands during the game; the University of Oregon also uses the tune, with different words
22. "On, Brave Old Army Team" (United States Military Academy)
    We don't want to forget the Army; a good song with one terrific passage
23. "Huskie Fight Song" (Northern Illinois University)
    Lively and very distinctive; can't ignore my own university
24. "Far Above Cayuga's Waters" (Cornell University)
    Really an alma mater rather than a fight song, but is such a collegiate classic, how can one overlook it? If played with a lively enough tempo, it becomes a relatively good fight song
25. "Our Director" (Harvard University/Rice University/Furman University)
    These three universities all use this excellent tune, but not always as a fight song; if the melody had a clearer identity with one institution, it would be in the top ten or fifteen (many other schools also use the tune, including the University of Southern California for its "Victory Song")

Honorable Mention

"War Eagle" (Auburn University)
"For Boston" (Boston College)
"Roar, Lion, Roar" (Columbia University)
"As the Backs Go Tearing By" (Dartmouth College)
"Duke Blue and White" (Duke University)
"The Gridiron King" (Harvard University)
"Big Red" (Lamar University)
"Michigan State Fight Song" (Michigan State University)
"Go U Northwestern" (Northwestern University)
"Le Regiment" (Ohio State University)

"The Nittany Lion" (Pennsylvania State University)
"The Princeton Cannon Song" (Princeton University)
"Come Join the Band" (Stanford University)
"Down, Down the Field" (Syracuse University)
"The Aggie War Hymn" (Texas A&M University)
"Roll On, Tulane" (Tulane University)
"Yea Alabama" (University of Alabama)
"Sing UCLA" (University of California, Los Angeles)
"Pride of the Illini" (University of Illinois at Urbana–Champaign)
"On, On, U of K" (University of Kentucky)
"Fight Tiger" (University of Missouri at Columbia)
"Dear Old Nebraska U" (University of Nebraska, Lincoln)
"Fight On, Pennsylvania" (University of Pennsylvania)
"Hail to Pitt" (University of Pittsburgh)
"Carolina Fight Song" (University of South Carolina)
"Bow Down to Washington" (University of Washington)
"Bingo, Eli Yale" (Yale University)

Special List of Institutions with Two or More Very Notable or Exceptional Songs, in Order of Superiority

1. Yale University ("Down the Field"; "Yale Boola"; "Bingo, Eli Yale")
2. Harvard University ("Our Director"; "The Gridiron King")
3. Ohio State University ("Across the Field"; "Le Regiment")
4. University of Illinois at Urbana–Champaign ("Illinois Loyalty"; "Pride of the Illini")

Historical Notes on the Songs
in This Collection

ALLEGHENY PEP SONG
(Allegheny College)

Brisk "Allegheny Pep Song" has been used as a fight song for the "Gold and Blue" of Allegheny College in Meadville, Pennsylvania. The anonymous song was copyrighted in 1924.

CHEER FOR OLD AMHERST
(Amherst College)

From Massachusetts to Ohio to California, that was the musical odyssey of Jason Noble Pierce (1880-1948). While a student at Amherst College in Amherst, Massachusetts, Pierce, class of 1902, wrote a fight song, "Cheer for Old Amherst," and copyrighted it in 1902. By the 1920s he wrote "Ten Thousand Strong," an alma mater for Oberlin College in Ohio. In 1936 he wrote "San Francisco Won My Heart" in honor of the city by the bay. Perhaps to help ensure his ultimate destination, he also published three small books on Christian theology for Pilgrim Press in 1912 and 1916.

GLORY, GLORY, TO OLD AMHERST
(Amherst College)

One could describe "Glory, Glory, to Old Amherst" as a drinking song, an alma mater, and/or a sports song. However, there is no uncertainty as to the source of the tune, the anonymous classic "The Battle Hymn of the Republic." The 1857 melody was arranged by

Norman Percy Foster, class of 1906, no later than 1906, and Foster may also have been the lyricist.

GLORY TO OLE AUBURN
(Auburn University)

Auburn University in Auburn, Alabama, is one of several large or famous universities that use the melody of "The Battle Hymn of the Republic" for a spirit or sports song. Among the other institutions that have adapted the anonymous masterpiece published in 1857 are the University of Georgia for its "Glory, Glory, to Old Georgia" and the University of Colorado for its "Glory, Glory, Colorado." The lyrics of the version still embraced by the "Tigers" or "War Eagles" of Auburn are anonymous. One of the university's sports nicknames, "War Eagles," is reflected in another current fight song, "War Eagle" (1955). That composition is among the better college songs of the post–World War II era, reflecting the talents of one of the better post–World War II songwriting teams, lyricist Al Stillman (1906-1979) and composer Robert Allen (1927-). They also collaborated on the strong standards "Chances Are" (1957) and "Home for the Holidays" (1954) as well as other enduring pieces.

FOR BOSTON
(Boston College)

Thomas J. Hurley, class of 1885, is not known for any notable achievement except for his vigorous and distinctive "For Boston," written for the "Eagles" of Boston College. The date of this fine song is uncertain, but the piece may well have been created in the 1880s, making it possibly one of the earliest compositions used as a fight song.

THE BROWN CHEERING SONG
(Brown University)

A lively jazzy composition, "The Brown Cheering Song" or "Cheering Song" was created by composer Howard Seth Young, class of 1908, and lyricist Robert Bradford Jones (1885-1948), class of 1907. Little is known about these two persons except for their authorship of this enduring piece.

EVER TRUE TO BROWN
(Brown University)

Ivy League member Brown University has a long tradition of student song, as reflected in at least three collections of campus songs that were published by the early 1920s. (These 1891, 1908, and 1921 anthologies, ranging from 73 to 120 pages in size, were all published under the title *Songs of Brown University*.) Around the time of the 1908 volume, a somewhat unconventional but effective sports song, "Ever True to Brown," was written for the Providence, Rhode Island, school. Donald Jackson, class of 1909, created both the words and music, apparently deriving the melody from his own march, "Emblem of Victory." The tune of "Ever True to Brown" is also used as the melody for "For Washburn and Her Team," a fight song of Washburn University in Topeka, Kansas.

FIGHT SONG
(Clemson University)

Although the legendary "Tiger Rag" (1917) has acquired lyrics since its initial composition, as used by the Mills Brothers in an early 1930s megahit recording, the "Tigers" of Clemson University in Clemson, South Carolina, have always performed their energetic "Fight Song" as a wordless instrumental version of the piece. The authorship of the jazz classic, however, is not as certain. Although the Original Dixieland Jazz Band has often been credited with the melody and Harry DeCosta with the lyrics, exactly who wrote the piece is far from certain. D. J. LaRocca and others have also been mentioned as possible creators of this very charming jewel for bands. Other schools also have used "Tiger Rag," including Livingston University in Livingston, Alabama, and Bethel College in North Newton, Kansas.

THE BIG RED TEAM
(Cornell University)

After the internationally famous "Far Above Cayuga's Waters," 1872 lyrics by Archibald C. Weeks and Wilmot M. Smith, 1858 melody by H. S. Thompson, the best known song at Cornell University in Ithaca, New York, is probably "The Big Red Team" or "Football Song." Written about 1905 by lyricist Romeyn Berry, class of 1904, and composer Charles E. Tourison, class of 1906, "The Big Red Team" is still heard on campus, supporting the sports teams of the "Big Red." Berry also turned his writing talents to books and magazines, including authoring a history of Cornell and an article which was reprinted by *Reader's Digest* in 1986, about eighty years after his noteworthy fight song writing effort. He also collaborated with the famous novelist Kenneth Lewis Roberts (1885-1957) on the story and lyrics for a comic opera, *Panatela,* presented on campus in 1907.

FIGHT FOR CORNELL
(Cornell University)

Around 1907, Theodore Julius Lindorff, class of 1907 at Cornell University, was very busy writing music. He was a contributor to the music for at least three comic operas presented at Cornell that year or soon after, and wrote the music for two university songs, "Carnelian and White" and "Fight for Cornell." The latter piece was created with the collaboration of lyricist Kenneth Lewis Roberts (1885-1957), class of 1908. In addition to collaborating on the circa 1907 fight song and one of the musicals, *Panatela* (1907), associated with Lindorff, Roberts wrote a series of American historical novels, including the notable *Northwest Passage* (1937) and *Captain Caution* (1934), which like his "Fight for Cornell" involved combat.

AS THE BACKS GO TEARING BY
(Dartmouth College)

This very good piece by lyricist John Thomas Keady, class of 1905, and composer Carl W. Blaisdell went energetically tearing from its origins at Dartmouth College in Hanover, New Hampshire, to the University of Cincinnati where the melody and modified lyrics are used as a fight song with the same title. Still reportedly used by the "Big Green" of Dartmouth, "As the Backs Go Tearing By" was created before 1907.

DUKE BLUE AND WHITE
(Duke University)

Whether it is called "Duke Blue and White," "Blue and White Fighting Song," or "Blue and White," it is a very good song for an outstanding university. G. E. Leftwich Jr. wrote the words and music, which were copyrighted in 1930, and the sports teams of the "Blue Devils" of Duke University in Durham, North Carolina, have used them ever since.

FORDHAM RAM
(Fordham University)

At one time, the "Rams" of Fordham University were regarded as an intercollegiate athletic power and therefore the tough and aggressive title "Fordham Ram" is an appropriate one for the sports programs of this well-respected Jesuit University in the Bronx, New York. John Ignatius Coveney, class of 1906, wrote this vigorous and dynamic composition in 1905. Coveney (1884?-1911) was a tackle on the 1905 Fordham football team as well as a talented musician who played several instruments. A bronze plaque on the Fordham campus memorializes the creator of the still-popular song, which is also referred to simply as "The Ram."

HAIL THE WHITE AND PURPLE
(Furman University)

The "Paladins" of Furman University in Greenville, South Carolina, use the trio (main section) of a famous march, "Our Director," as the melody for their fight song "Hail the White and Purple." This outstanding piece of music, written by Frederick Ellsworth Bigelow (1873-1929) in 1895, is also used for "Our Director," a fight song of Harvard University, and for "Rice's Honor," the fight-song style alma mater of Rice University. The lyrics of "Hail the White and Purple," sometimes called "Hail to White and Purple" are anonymous.

SONS OF GEORGETOWN
(Georgetown University)

Despite having the literary style of an alma mater, this strong, expansive march could serve as an effective fight song. Apparently still used by the "Hoyas" of Georgetown University in Washington, DC, "Sons of Georgetown" combines lyrics by Robert T. Collier, class of 1894, with an anonymous tune. Collier also wrote the words for Georgetown's official alma mater "Hail! O Georgetown," also set to an anonymous melody. Another fight song for District of Columbia university is "The Flying Cardinals," written for the Catholic University of America around 1938 by Paul D. H. Leman, bandmaster at the time. Apparently, this composition was little used.

HARVARDIANA
(Harvard University)

Although no longer an official fight song, jazzy "Harvardiana" remains popular on the campus in Cambridge, Massachusetts. The composition was written in 1909 by composer Raymond George Williams (1887-) and lyricist S. B. Steel, both of the class of 1911, and served as a primary fight song for the "Crimson" for many years after. Williams, who composed a few other pieces, was later manager of the Rhode Island Philharmonic and the Boston Symphony Orchestra.

TEN THOUSAND MEN OF HARVARD
(Harvard University)

There are probably not 10,000 men who have performed in the Harvard University Band since its premiere at Soldiers Field in

Chicago in 1919. But this famous and innovative ensemble, one of only three student-managed college bands in the United States (along with the University of California at Berkeley and Stanford University), has probably performed the striking "Ten Thousand Men of Harvard" many hundreds of times. The 1914 composition was written by composer Murray Taylor and lyricist A. Putnam, both of the class of 1918. Also known as "10,000 Men," it received a fine band arrangement from the talented hands of celebrated composer Leroy Anderson (1908-1975), of the class of 1929.

FOOTBALL SONG
(Haverford College)

Haverford College in Haverford, Pennsylvania, has a "Football Song" and at least one famous graduate. Elliot Field (1875-), class of 1897, wrote this sports song, which was copyrighted in 1902. He also edited the *Haverford College Song Book* (1903), and wrote at least twenty plays in the 1930s and 1940s. That is, he went from football plays to stage plays.

INDIANA FIGHT!
(Indiana University)

Although not as famous as "Indiana, Our Indiana," 1911 music by Karl L. King, 1912 lyrics by Russell P. Harker, "Indiana Fight!" well serves the fight song appetites of the "Hoosiers" of Indiana University in Bloomington. "Indiana Fight!" was written in 1923 by Leroy C. Hinkle, class of 1923.

FIGHT FOR LSU
(Louisiana State University)

Castro Carazo (1895-) is a significant figure in the musical history of Louisiana. Born in San José, Costa Rica, Carazo conducted military bands there and also led the New Orleans Federal

Symphony and the Louisiana State University Concert Band in Baton Rouge. In addition to wielding a baton, he composed several works for symphony orchestra and band, including the tune for the official fight song of the university, "Fight for LSU." Published in 1937, the piece was accompanied by lyrics by W. G. "Hickey" Higgenbotham. Carazo also wrote the music for two other LSU songs, "Darling of LSU" and "Touchdown for LSU," both published in 1935. The lyricist for these two compositions was none other than the legendary Louisiana politician, Huey Pierce Long (1893-1935). A less famous contributor to LSU music is Gene Quaw, who wrote the lyrics for another fight song "Hey, Fightin' Tigers," as well as creating some other songs in the 1920s. The melody used for "Hey, Fightin' Tigers" is the tune written by Cy Coleman for the Lucille Ball number "Hey, Look Me Over" in the 1960 musical *Wildcat*. Yet another musical cat associated with the "Tigers" of Louisiana State is the 1926 fight song "Bengal Swing," by Elizabeth K. MacMillan, class of 1925.

SONS OF MARSHALL
(Marshall University)

"Sons of Marshall" does not refer to the offspring of the long time Chief Justice of the United States John Marshall (1755-1835). Instead it refers to the students of Marshall University in Huntington, West Virginia, which was founded in 1837 as Marshall Academy in honor of the very influential jurist. One of these students, Ralph A. Williams, attended the then Marshall College in 1907 and wrote "Sons of Marshall" in 1935 in honor of the college and his daughter Dorothy Grace Williams. The composition is now the official fight song of the "Thundering Herd," which has recently thundered over many opponents in football.

OH! DIDN'T HE RAMBLE
(New Mexico State University)

The "Aggies" of New Mexico State University probably hope to ramble across the opposition's goal line many times, in line with their fight song, "Oh! Didn't He Ramble." The words and music to this lively 1902 piece are by the celebrated African-American composer W. C. (William Christopher) Handy (1873-1958), who is internationally famous for his 1914 jazz classic "St. Louis Blues." The 1902 song is also called "Aggies Fight Song" on the Las Cruces campus, where it is usually performed as an instrumental. The same tune is used at Princeton University for its "Ramble Song."

OLD NEW YORK UNIVERSITY
(New York University)

There have been at least two editions of the *New York University Song Book,* one published in 1915 and a greatly expanded volume issued in 1942. Among the compositions included in the earlier edition was a noteworthy song with the pleasantly sentimental title "Old New York University." In spite of the alma-mater style title, this piece has served as the fight song of the prestigious private university located in the Washington Square area of Manhattan, where it has been given the generic title, "The Fight Song." Its words and music were written by R. W. Ferns, class of 1909, who is otherwise very obscure. Another sports song at NYU is "Fight for Your Violet."

OBERLIN PEP SONG
(Oberlin College)

A smaller institution with notable music programs, Oberlin College in Oberlin, Ohio, has produced at least two fight songs. In 1923 "Oberlin Pep Song," a lively alma-mater style tribute to the school, was copyrighted. The words and music were written by composer, choirmaster, and organist Rob Roy Peery (1900-1973), who also compiled and arranged several classical compositions in his 1965 *Rob Roy Peery All Classic Duet Book* for organ and piano, as well as composing cantatas and instrumental works and working for music publishers. In 1946 another Oberlin song, "A Song of Victory," was copyrighted. Its lyrics were by John Prindle Scott and its melody was derived from the 1931 march "Down the Street" by Victor Grabel (1886-1965).

THE BUCKEYE BATTLE CRY
(Ohio State University)

One of the battle cries, or, if you prefer, fight songs used by the "Buckeyes" of Ohio State University in Columbus is "The Buckeye Battle Cry." Copyrighted in 1919, this very good composition was created by Frank Crumit (1889-1943), probably around 1910. In addition to writing the words and music for this enduring sports piece, Crumit wrote a number of other songs during the 1920s and 1930s, including "Ace in the Hole," a 1934 fox trot. Crumit's artistic partners on the 1934 song were Bartley Costello (1871-1941), a slightly notable songwriter, and Thomas "Fats" Waller (1904-1943), the famous jazz composer.

OHIO STATE
(Ohio State University)

Now mostly forgotten among Ohio State University's excellent musical heritage is the fight song "Ohio State" or "Ohio State March Song," copyrighted in 1912. Ray W. Arms, class of 1912, wrote this piece for the "Buckeyes."

RALLY, OHIO!
(Ohio State University)

With its spoken "locomotive" at the end and its sung exhortation for the team to rally, "Rally, Ohio!" is a charming college composition. Written in 1916 by Philip M. Foote, Ohio State University class of 1919, it is a fine example of college spirit in that era. Both a lyricist and composer, Foote published several other songs during the 1930s, sometimes writing only the music, as well as doing some arranging.

FIGHT ON, STATE
(Pennsylvania State University)

This official fight song of Pennsylvania State University, part of a noteworthy body of song at the school, was written in 1915 and has been entirely credited to Joe Saunders, about whom little is known except that he was a member of the class of 1915. While Saunders was definitely the creator of the superior melody, there is good reason to believe that F. E. Wilbur, not Saunders, was the author of the lyrics.

THE NITTANY LION
(Pennsylvania State University)

There is only one known song with the title "The Nittany Lion." Bright, bubbly, bouncy, and brassy, the exceptional composition by James Leyden helps cheer on the often exceptional athletics teams of the "Nittany Lions" of Pennsylvania State University in University Park. However, there may have been two popular-culture musicians named James Leyden. The person who wrote "The Nittany Lion," James A. Leyden, was a member of the class of 1914 and most likely was born in the early 1890s. That piece and two others written by Leyden for the university, "Victory" and "PSC (Pennsylvania State College) March," were published in 1919. "Nittany" and "Victory" both remain popular on the campus today. If there was a second James Leyden, he was born in 1921, possibly was the son of the first James Leyden, coauthored several musicals, and was a group vocal recording artist.

VICTORY
(Pennsylvania State University)

Perhaps having the most candid one-word title possible for a fight song, "Victory" is a still-performed exhortation to the men and women who represent Pennsylvania State University in sports. This good march was written by James A. Leyden, class of 1914, and published in 1919 along with another attractive Penn State composition by him, "The Nittany Lion." A later song created for the school is "Hail! Oh Hail," by Ray T. Fortunato, class of 1947, who became an administrator at his alma mater and a published expert on college personnel management.

THE ORANGE AND THE BLACK
(Princeton University)

There are at least two songs with "orange" and "black" in their titles which have been used by the "Tigers" of Princeton University. In 1924, Mayhew Lester Lake (1879-1955), a prolific band composer, published his march, "Orange and Black." By 1894, Clarence B. Mitchell, class of 1889, wrote the lyrics for "The Orange and the Black," which were set to a tune, "Sadie Ray," written around 1870 by J. Tannenbaum. "The Orange and the Black," a march that is at least to some degree a fight song, was still quite active in the late 1960s on the campus in Princeton, New Jersey.

THE PRINCETON CANNON SONG
(Princeton University)

"The Princeton Cannon Song," also known as "The Princeton Canon Song March," "The Cannon Song," and even "Princeton Canon Song," is a finely-crafted jewel from this prestigious New Jersey university. The official fight song of the "Tigers," it was written in 1906 by composer Arthur H. "Rag" Osborn, class of 1907, and lyricist Joseph F. Hewitt, also of the class of 1907. The song was printed in the original volume of *College Fight Songs* in a recent arrangement and without words, but the high quality of the composition justifies another printing here, using the original form of the melody and the original lyrics.

PRINCETON FORWARD MARCH
(Princeton University)

Kenneth S. Clark (1882-1943), class of 1905, wrote several fight songs for the "Tigers" of Princeton University. He created the words and music for "Princeton Jungle March" (1904), the words for "Ramble Song" (around 1904 or 1905), and the words and music for "Princeton Forward March," which was published in 1914. He also served in World War I (as possibly predicted by his "Forward March"), was a businessman after the war, and wrote a variety of other songs for popular consumption.

PRINCETON JUNGLE MARCH
(Princeton University)

The "Jungle" in "Princeton Jungle March" refers to the Princeton Tiger, the school's mascot. Also known as "The Princeton Jungle," this lively piece was conceived by Kenneth S. Clark (1882-1943), who was born in Pittsburgh and who graduated from Princeton University in 1905. Clark wrote other songs for the Princeton, New Jersey, institution, including "Princeton Forward March" (1914), and "Ramble Song" (around 1904 or 1905).

RAMBLE SONG
(Princeton University)

In 1902, the celebrated jazz composer W. C. (William Christopher) Handy (1873-1958) wrote his first significant song, "Oh! Didn't He Ramble." Soon after, around 1904 or 1905, a Princeton University student, Kenneth S. Clark (1882-1943), wrote new lyrics to replace the original words by Handy. The result was the playful "Ramble Song." Another university utilizing Handy's dandy music for a fight song is New Mexico State University, which usually performs its "Oh! Didn't He Ramble" without words.

HAIL, PURDUE
(Purdue University)

When composer Edward J. Wotawa (1888-1963) class of 1912, and lyricist James Morrison, class of 1915, collaborated on this song in 1912, they called it "The Purdue War Song." When published in 1913, the composition's name was changed to the more timid "Hail, Purdue," and with that title the piece has since remained the pride of the "Boilermakers" of the renowned university in West Lafayette, Indiana. Versatile Wotawa, who like Morrison was a graduate of the School of Science, was a chemistry and physics teacher in a Louisville, Kentucky, high school for over a decade, and then became the head of the music department at the University of Louisville and a part-time violinist and violist with the Louisville Orchestra. The city of Louisville had good reason to proclaim "Hail, Wotawa" for quite a while. A few years before Wotawa wrote "Hail, Purdue," around 1910, Paul S. Emrick (1884-1961), class of 1908, returned to his alma mater to teach electrical engineering and direct the band. Before he retired in 1954, he had made a number of band innovations, and had produced several marches for the school. These include "Greater Purdue March" (1923) and still sometimes performed "Fighting Varsity" (1920s?).

COME JOIN THE BAND
(Stanford University)

The fact that Stanford University is one of only three American universities that has a student-managed band has not seemed to discourage students from joining the band, as suggested by the cream of Stanford songs, "Come Join the Band." (The other two universities are Harvard University and the University of California at Berkeley.) A combination of a fine melody, "New Colonial March," written in 1895 by Robert Browne Hall (1858-1907), and good lyrics, written in 1907 by Aurania Ellerbeck, have blended into one of the better college compositions. Ellerbeck (1885-), class of 1909, was reportedly inspired to create the words the night of a rally which preceded the "big game" of 1907. Later on, Ellerbeck, under her married name Aurania Ellerbeck Rouverol, was inspired to write at least three plays, *Love Isn't Everything* (1937) (with Émile Littler), *Where the Heart Is* (1941), and *The Great American Family* (1947). She also was associated with the Century Play Company in New York City. Among the other sports songs written for the "Cardinal" of Stanford have been "When Stanford Begins to Score," by W. A. Irwin, class of 1899, "Victory Song" by G. H. Yost, class of 1900, "Just Because They Hit That Line So Hard," by M. A. Thomas Jr., class of 1904, "The Cardinal Song" (1903), by Alice Kimball, class of 1904, "Sons of Stanford Red" (1909), by William Achi, class of 1911, and Geoffrey F. Morgan, class of 1909, and "The Cardinal Is Waving" (1915), by William G. Paul, class of 1917.

DOWN, DOWN THE FIELD
(Syracuse University)

Although also known by the name "Down the Field," the same title as the more famous Yale University song, this very good composition is usually referred to by the title "Down, Down the Field" to avoid confusion with the Yale piece. (The first four words of the lyrics are actually, "Down, down the field.") "Down, Down the Field" was created in 1914 by composer C. Harold Lewis and lyricist Ralph Murphy, both of the class of 1915. It has served the "Orangemen" of Syracuse University quite well since then, helping to keep the teams and fans up, up.

THE SALTINE WARRIOR
(Syracuse University)

With its provocative title, "The Saltine Warrior" was a strident sports song for the "Orangemen" of Syracuse University for a number of years after its composition around 1912. This very interesting piece, which has nothing to do with a snack cracker but instead figuratively cracks the whip on the university's sports teams, was created by lyricist Samuel E. Darby Jr., class of 1913, and musician David R. Walsh, class of 1912.

THE AGGIE WAR HYMN
(Texas A&M University)

"The Aggie War Hymn," also known by the more specific title "Texas Aggie War Hymn," is an enthusiastic exhortation to sports victory for the "Aggies" in College Station. Published in 1921, it was the creation of J. V. "Pinky" Wilson, class of 1920, who is obscure. Around 1950 the piece was one of four A&M songs honored by being recorded on a two-disc, 78 rpm album with the title *Songs of Texas A&M*. Generally better known than "The Aggie War Hymn" is "Jalisco," the composition adopted as the fight song of Texas A&M University at Kingsville, formerly known as Texas A&I University. Since that campus is not far from the Mexican border, it is not at all surprising that they favor the Mexican flavor of the fine collaboration by lyricist Ernesto M. Cortázar and musician Manuel Esperon, which was published in Mexico in 1941 under the title "Ay! Jalisco, no te rajes" ("Don't Chatter, Jalisco").

BROWN AND BLUE FOREVER
(Tufts University)

Written in 1916 when Tufts University was called Tufts College, "Brown and Blue Forever" was the collaboration of lyricist E. A. Terhune, class of 1917, and composer N. W. Morison, class of 1916. Of course, in those good old days before contemporary sports equipment, the players for the "Brown and Blue" often got quite black and blue in football games on the campus in Medford, Massachusetts.

SEMPER PARATUS
(United States Coast Guard Academy)

If you have watched the annual televised Memorial Day concerts from the Capitol grounds in Washington, DC, you have heard rousing "Semper Paratus" ("Always Ready") as the opening number of the stirring "Armed Forces Medley." The song was published in 1928, after the death of its creator, Captain Francis Saltus Van Boskerck (1868-1927), an officer at the Coast Guard Academy in New London, Connecticut. It has for many years been the beloved fight song of the Academy as well as the musical symbol of the United States Coast Guard. This brilliant gem is one of the finest sports songs from a smaller institution. A medium-sized school that uses the tune of "Semper Paratus" is Sam Houston State University in Huntsville, Texas, whose "Fight Song" is set to the same exciting melody.

YEA, ALABAMA
(University of Alabama)

His nickname was "Epp," and he produced an *E*specially *P*eppy *Piece*. Ethelred Lundy (Epp) Sykes, at the time editor of the school newspaper, wrote "Yea, Alabama" for a 1926 contest sponsored by the school magazine. The exuberant composition became the official fight song or musical general of the "Crimson Tide" of the University of Alabama in Tuscaloosa, and Sykes eventually became a military Brigadier General in the Air Force. That is, a first-rate song for a first-rate football power came from an apparently first-rate person.

FIGHT! WILDCATS! FIGHT!
(University of Arizona)

"Fight! Wildcats! Fight!," also known as "Fight, Wild Cats, Fight," is the collaborative effort of two moderately famous persons. The creators of this good sports song used by the "Wildcats" of the University of Arizona in Tucson, however, received most of their renown from other activities. Cocomposer Thornton Whitney Allen (1890-1944), born in Newark, New Jersey, was a legend in college music circles. He composed or cocomposed several notable fight songs and founded two significant publishing firms that specialized in printing college songs, including this one, which was copyrighted in 1930. Douglas S. Holsclaw (1898-1995), the cocomposer and lyricist, was a 1925 graduate of the university, plus a businessman, philanthropist, playwright, Arizona state legislator from 1953-1975, and a Tucson community activist.

RAZORBACK PEP SONG
(University of Arkansas)

Of some historical importance to the University of Arkansas in Fayetteville are two fight songs by William M. Paisley, class of 1925. Paisley wrote the words and music for "Razorback Pep Song," copyrighted 1924, and the music for "Razorback Rootin' Song" (1931). Jewel Hughes and Catherine Walker wrote the lyrics for the 1931 composition. The current fight song is "Arkansas Fight," by Joel T. Leach, whose first known publication was written in 1972.

BIG C
(University of California at Berkeley)

Originally, the "C" in "Big C" represented both the University of California at Berkeley and the large Cement third letter of the alphabet built on the "rugged eastern foothills" of the campus in 1905. Eventually, the "C" also came to signify a controversy over copyright with another state school, UCLA. In 1913, composer Harold P. Williams and lyricist Norman Loyall McLaren, both of the class of 1914, entered their tribute to the 1905 campus symbol in the annual school song contest, which they won. In the 1960s, F. Kelley James, formerly a member of the Cal Band and at the time Associate Director of the band at the University of California, Los Angeles, created an arrangement of "Big C" for a joint half-time show which included performances by the bands of Cal, UCLA, and two other schools. Later, the UCLA Band added its own set of lyrics to "Big C"'s brisk melody, renamed the piece "Sons of Westwood," and made it one of their fight songs. Cal was understandably upset over this borrowing by a rival, but since the 1913 composition was never copyrighted, "Big C" was legally as well as artistically big enough to be a significant fight song for two major universities. UCLA had a number of good fight songs by the 1960s, including "Go On, Bruins" (copyright 1944) by Gordon J. Holmquist, Milo Sweet, and Gwen Sweet, along with others in the 1948 edition of *Songs of UCLA,* so their acquisition of "Big C" is a definite compliment to the quality of the Cal song.

CALIFORNIA INDIAN SONG
(University of California at Berkeley)

Before the sports nickname of Stanford University became the "Cardinal," it was the "Indians." Therefore, this circa 1907 composition by Harold W. Bingham, class of 1906, refers to the long-standing rivalry between the Stanford "Indians" and the "Golden Bears" of the University of California at Berkeley. The verses, which simulate a war chant, are seldom performed today, but the chorus is still actively used. Bingham also wrote Cal's official alma mater, "All Hail! Blue and Gold," in 1905, and penned other school songs.

SONS OF CALIFORNIA
(University of California at Berkeley)

Part of the rich musical heritage of the University of California at Berkeley are two songs by Clinton Ralza Morse, class of 1896. In 1907, pianist and glee club organizer "Brick" Morse wrote an alma mater, "Hail to California," which is almost as beloved as Cal's official alma mater, "All Hail! Blue and Gold." "Hail to California" is also used as the alma mater at the University of California, Davis, the University of California, Los Angeles, the University of California, Santa Barbara, and other state universities. The campus at Davis also uses the popular Berkeley fight songs "Big C" (1913), by composer Harold P. Williams and lyricist Norman Loyall McLaren, and "Sons of California" (1905), the second enduring composition by Morse. One of the reasons for the continuing usage of "Sons" is a faster tempo arrangement made during the late 1930s, replacing Morse's original less lively glee club style. Morse also compiled the 1919 edition of *Songs of California,* and produced *California Football History,* a substantial 1937 volume on Cal gridiron accomplishments.

THE STANFORD JONAH
(University of California at Berkeley)

One of the cleverest of college songs, "The Stanford Jonah" was written in 1913 by Ted E. Haley, class of 1915. It was submitted as an entry in the annual school song contest that year, but lost to another top Cal song, "Big C." However, it won in 1914, and has continued to be a favorite, partly because of its reference to Cal's "Golden Bear" swallowing rival Stanford University as in the story of Jonah. Similar concept songs reportedly have been used at Georgia Institute of Technology and the United States Naval Academy.

FIGHT CU, DOWN THE FIELD
(University of Colorado)

Although the official fight song of the University of Colorado in Boulder is not long in performing time, it appears to have been written by the 1920s and therefore is long in durability. The words for "Fight CU, Down the Field" were created by obscure Richard Durnett, and were set to an old tune used by the Culver Military Academy. Another Colorado state university is the University of Northern Colorado in Greeley. The "Bears," a regional football powerhouse in the 1990s, are represented musically by "UNC Fight Song," the anonymous lyrics of which are given below:

On down the field we go to victory,

The colors navy blue & gold.

And to our fighting team we hold

Our spirit high.

The mighty Bears are we . . . GO BEARS!!

Fight, fight to win each battle fairly,

The only way we e're shall be,

We shout out the name,

To keep the fame and glory to old U-N-C!!

(Used by permission of the University of Northern Colorado)

GLORY, GLORY, COLORADO
(University of Colorado)

Like its counterpart, "Glory, Glory, to Old Georgia," favored by the University of Georgia, "Glory, Glory, Colorado" uses a very appropriate tune for intercollegiate competition. With the rousing 1857 melody of "The Battle Hymn of the Republic" accompanying its athletic teams, the "Buffaloes" of the University of Colorado in Boulder can hope for many glorious victories. The anonymous words for this unofficial fight song were written before the 1930s. Unlike "Glory, Glory, to Old Georgia," which uses just the refrain of the great hymn, "Glory, Glory, Colorado" uses the entire melody.

THE ORANGE AND BLUE
(University of Florida)

Thornton Whitney Allen (1890-1944), wrote a variety of college songs, including the famous "Washington and Lee Swing" (1910), for which he helped with the melody. One such composition is "The Orange and Blue," also know as "On, Brave Old Florida!," The pep song of the "Gators" of the University of Florida in Gainesville. Allen wrote the music and the words for the verses, and George Hamilton wrote the words for the refrain, which is sometimes the only section performed. Note that this piece, copyrighted in 1925, does not mention alligators. However, another Florida song by Allen, "March of the Fighting Gators," has the swamp creatures prominently in the title.

CHEER ILLINI
(University of Illinois at Urbana-Champaign)

Written about the same time as the famous "Illinois Loyalty" (1906) by Thatcher Howland Guild, "Cheer Illini" was copyrighted in 1912. Composer Harold V. Hill, class of 1911, and lyricist Howard R. Green, class of 1912, collaborated on the piece. Green also wrote a play, *The Plympton Blood,* in 1934.

ILLINOIS LOYALTY
(University of Illinois at Urbana-Champaign)

Smooth and transporting "Illinois Loyalty," with its trademark opening lines, "We're loyal to you, Illinois, We're orange and blue,

Illinois," is sufficiently beloved at the University of Illinois that when Carl Clive Burford wrote a history of the university's bands in 1952, the book's title was *We're Loyal to You, Illinois*. This official fight song was written for the "Illini" in 1906, under the title "We're Loyal to You, Illinois," by Thatcher Howland Guild (1879-1914). A cornet player, Guild came to the campus in 1904 and was still living in Urbana at the time of his very premature death. He is not known to have published any other musical compositions, but he did write at least ten plays for the theater.

I'M A JAYHAWK
(University of Kansas)

Perhaps the second most popular fight song ever used at the University of Kansas is "I'm a Jayhawk." (Its tune is also popular on other campuses, including reportedly being used for the fight song "Stand Up and Cheer" at Alabama A&M University in Normal.) Written by George H. Bowles, class of 1911, probably around 1910 but not copyrighted until 1920, "I'm a Jayhawk" is an energetic companion to the fine "Stand Up and Cheer" (1909) by Paul P. McNeely, class of 1910. Incidentally, there are a number of fans who follow both the "Jayhawks" of the University of Kansas in Lawrence and the "Wildcats" of Kansas State University in Manhattan. These dual-team persons are called "Jaycats." The followers of another state university in Kansas, Wichita State University, sing the anonymous "Hail, Wichita," believed to have been written in 1962. The lyrics for the fight song of the "Shockers" are given below:

> All Hail, Hail, Wichita
>
> U Rah, Rah, Rah, for Wichita
>
> March onward, banners high
>
> With courage, force that
>
> can never die. (Rah)
>
> We'll fight for Wichita

Brave spirits never fail

To Wichita all loyalty

Hail our Varsity triumphantly, Hail

(Used by permission)

HAIL TO U OF L
(University of Louisville)

This attractive march, with mention of "shouts and cheering" plus "glorious vict'ries," is a suitable sports song in spite of the reference to "alma mater." Published in 1924, it was written by George A. Resta (who became a physician), and was actively performed until at least the 1950s. A later song, "UL Fight Song" by Robert B. Griffith, is currently used by the "Cardinals" of the University of Louisville. Another fight song that has been a favorite at Louisville is Milo Sweet's "On! You Cardinals."

MARYLAND, MY MARYLAND
(University of Maryland)

Although not the official fight song of the "Terrapins" of the University of Maryland in College Park, this stately anthem has been employed as a sports composition. The familiar melody, first used for the possibly sixteenth- or seventeenth-century German carol, "O Tannenbaum," became the tune for the state's official song, "Maryland, My Maryland," after James Ryder Randall (1839-1908) wrote a set of fervent patriotic lyrics in 1861. By the early twentieth century, the Maryland campus had also appropriated the tune and Randall's words, but usually only the third verse, which begins "Thou wilt not cower in the dust," was sung at sporting events.

GO! TIGERS, GO!
(University of Memphis)

With a song title like "Go! Tigers, Go!," there is little doubt as to the sports nickname of the University of Memphis. This enthusiastic composition was written in 1961, when the university's name was Memphis State University. Its creators were musician Thomas C. Ferguson (1932-) and lyricist Edwin Hubbard (1935-1997). After the university changed its name to its present form, the lyrics were slightly modified in 1994, with the original line "Shout for dear old MSU" altered to "Shout for dear old Memphis U."

VARSITY
(University of Michigan)

For many years he was mister music at the University of Michigan. Earl Vincent Moore (1890-1987), class of 1912, was professor of music at the Ann Arbor campus from 1923 to 1946, and dean of the music school from 1946 to 1960. While a student there in 1911, he wrote the music for "Varsity," a very good long-term sports song for the "Wolverines." (J. Fred Lawton, class of 1911, wrote the lyrics.) Moore also wrote two 1909 alma-mater style songs for Michigan, "College Days" with lyricist Donald A. Kahn, and "Michigan, Goodbye," with lyricists Kahn and Lawton. He was also a major contributor to several musicals and other extended vocal works and helped edit several editions of *Michigan's Favorite College Songs* between 1913 and 1940.

WIN FOR MICHIGAN
(University of Michigan)

William T. Whedon, an 1881 graduate of the University of Michigan, wrote one of the earliest songs used on the Ann Arbor campus. The sports march "Win for Michigan" was most likely written around 1881, but was not copyrighted until 1913.

TIGER SONG OF U OF M
(University of Missouri at Columbia)

One of the earliest fight songs at the University of Missouri at Columbia was "Tiger Song of U of M," copyrighted in 1916. Its author was Preston Kendall, who also wrote an early alma mater, "Mid the Hills of Old Missouri," in 1908. The present fight song of the "Tigers" is "Fight, Tiger," by lyricist Donald M. MacKay and composer Robert F. Karsch, a piece with much energy, perhaps so designed to easily traverse the hills of mid-Missouri.

NORTH DAKOTA U
(University of North Dakota)

Although the original title of this song, copyrighted in 1921, was "North Dakota U," it is perhaps better known as "It's for You, North Dakota U," the composition's most memorable line. The creator of the piece was Franz Rickaby, who died in 1925 after an apparently short life which included the compilation of two song collections, *The Songs of Knox College* (1916) and *Ballads and Songs of the Shanty-Boy* (1926, reprinted 1993). It is reportedly still heard on the campus in Grand Forks, along with the official fight song, "Fight on, Sioux," written before 1950 by Raymond "Aimee" Johnson.

FIGHT, NORTH TEXAS
(University of North Texas)

Francis E. Stroup apparently had an affinity for universities with "North" in their names. In 1939, while an intercollegiate athlete, he wrote the words and music for lively "Fight, North Texas," the official fight song of the "Green and White" of North Texas State University in Denton, now the University of North Texas. Twenty-two years later, while a physical education professor at Northern Illinois University, he revised the chorus of a tune written much earlier by music professor A. Neil Annas, added some lyrics, and produced the peppy 1961 "Huskie Fight Song" for the Illinois university. When North Texas played Northern Illinois in football in 1996, it was one of those very rare occasions when the opposing teams in a Division IA game used official fight songs by the same person. The two universities also have something else in common—nationally notable music programs.

MIGHTY OREGON
(University of Oregon)

Also known as "The Tipperary of the West" (a reference to "It's a Long, Long Way to Tipperary," the celebrated 1912 British composition by Jack Judge (1878-1938) and Harry Williams (d. 1930) which was a World War I favorite), "Mighty Oregon" is the official fight song of the "Ducks" of the University of Oregon in Eugene during all gridiron battles. Composer Albert Perfect and lyricist DeWitt Gilbert published this good march in 1916. Other Perfect pieces include two compositions of uncertain date, "Swedish Fest March" and "Two Little Chums."

CHEER PENNSYLVANIA
(University of Pennsylvania)

This is one of the few instances in which one person wrote enduring fight songs for two different major colleges or universities. Caleb W. O'Connor, a 1904 graduate of Yale University who wrote the lyrics for Yale's famous 1904 "Down the Field," created the words and music for "Cheer Pennsylvania" in 1906. The later song is still used at the University of Pennsylvania in Philadelphia, a longtime Yale rival in the prestigious Ivy League.

FIGHT ON, PENNSYLVANIA
(University of Pennsylvania)

"Fight On, Pennsylvania," one of the better college compositions, was written for the "Penn Quakers" in 1923. The words for this official sports song of the University of Pennsylvania were by Ben S. McGiveran, class of 1923, and the music was by David Zoob, also of the same class. The fighting tone of the piece, typical of its genre, may seem to be inconsistent with the well-known pacifism of the Quakers.

THE PITT PANTHER
(University of Pittsburgh)

Pittsburgh, Panthers, and Panella were closely linked together for over a generation. Louis J. Panella (1881-1940) was born and died in Pittsburgh, Pennsylvania, performed with the Pittsburgh Symphony Orchestra, and taught trumpet for twenty-six years at Pittsburgh's Carnegie Institute of Technology (now Carnegie Mellon University). He also wrote the music for "The Pitt Panther" (1922), one of over 200 marches and popular songs with which he was involved. Howard E. Reppert, class of 1923, wrote the lyrics to Panella's fight song for the "Panthers" of the University of Pittsburgh. Panella also wrote "The University of Dayton" (1925), also known as "UD Loyalty March," for the University of Dayton. Reppert also wrote the lyrics for "Billy Pitt" (around 1923) to go with a march melody by C.V. Starrett, class of 1924. In a sense "Billy Pitt" is a fight song, referring to an eighteenth-century conflict between the British and Indians.

PITTSBURGH'S BIG TEAM
(University of Pittsburgh)

George Morrill Kirk, class of 1912, is perhaps best known for creating the lyrics to "Hail to Pitt" (1910), the official fight song of the University of Pittsburgh. The melody of the 1910 composition is by Lester M. Taylor. However, Kirk also wrote both the words and music for another Pitt march, "Pittsburgh's Big Team," which was copyrighted in 1916. Among the Pitt fight songs not by Kirk are "The Panther" (copyright 1927), "The Battle Song" (copyright 1925), and "Chant" or "School Chant" (around 1915), all three by lyricist Horace C. Scott, dental school class of 1915, and composer C.S. Harris, dental school class of 1916. Other sports pieces in the plentiful Pittsburgh repertory are "Pitt Fight Song," by Kenneth N. McKee, class of 1925, "Fight, Fight, Fight!," by Richard M. Skidmore, medical school class of 1931, "Cheer for the Dear Old Lady," lyrics by "G.M. P.B.," class of 1909, music by "E.S.," class of 1921, and two probably pre-1920s anonymous compositions, "Fight for Pittsburgh" and "O-O-O-O."

RHODE ISLAND CHEER SONG
(University of Rhode Island)

Frank K. Baxter, class of 1914, wrote the words and music of "Rhode Island Cheer Song" for Rhode Island State College, now the University of Rhode Island. Probably seldom used today by the "Rams" at the campus in Kingston, the composition was copyrighted in 1922.

CAROLINA FIGHT SONG
(University of South Carolina)

Striking "Carolina Fight Song," which has definite touches of pomp and majesty, is a splendid representative of the University of South Carolina in Columbia. It was written in 1933, in response to a contest for a new fight song, by Carrere Salley. First used in the 1950s, replacing "The NC-4," it in turn was replaced by yet another fight song in 1968, becoming the "Old Fight Song." It is still performed, to enthusiastic fan response, in the Marching Band's pregame ceremonies along with the current official fight song, "The Fighting Gamecocks Lead the Way," a more typical bouncy and active sports song. The arrangement for the version of "Carolina Fight Song" printed in this volume is by James D. Pritchard (1920-), Director of Bands from 1959 to 1969. Pritchard, later a professor and associate director of the School of Music, also wrote the 1962 lyrics for USC's "Fight for Victory," which is set to the melody of "This Game" (1961) by the notable American popular composer Gordon Jenkins (1910-1984). The words to "Fight for Victory" are given below:

> Fight, Fight for vict'ry
>
> We pledge our loyalty, gamecocks
>
> Come on let's cheer for the garnet and black
>
> Yes, we are for the fighting gamecocks.
>
> Fight, Team, Fight!
>
> 'Cause USC is best of all

And vict'ry will be ours today

Yes, we're from Carolina, USC

We'll fight for vict'ry today.

Permission was authorized in 1964 by Leeds Music Corp. for the University of South Carolina Band to use these words with their publication "This Game," composed and arranged by Gordon Jenkins (circa 1961).

FIGHT! USC
(University of South Carolina)

It was perhaps natural for a Marine recruiting sergeant stationed in Columbia, South Carolina, to write a brisk military-style song such as "Fight! USC." George Tideman (1930-) created the very good piece in 1966 for the University of South Carolina band.

THE FIGHTING GAMECOCK SONG
(University of South Carolina)

"The Fighting Gamecock Song," a lively piece, was written in 1967 for the "Gamecocks" of the University of South Carolina by E. B. "Buzz" Purcell, an attorney. Another fight song with "Gamecock" in its title is "The Gamecocks of South Carolina U" (1940), by Fred Waring (1900-1984), Tom Waring (1902-1960), and Francis Drake "Pat" Ballard (1899-1960). That trio of composers wrote a number of mostly forgotten fight songs around that time.

THE FIGHTING GAMECOCKS LEAD THE WAY
(University of South Carolina)

The current official sports song of the University of South Carolina is "The Fighting Gamecocks Lead the Way." Its lyrics were written in 1968 by Paul Dietzel, football coach from 1966 to 1974. The music was arranged in 1968 by the then Director of Bands

James D. Pritchard, from the number "Step to the Rear," a highlight of the 1967 Broadway musical *How Now, Dow Jones.* The creator of the lively original melody is the eminent American film composer Elmer Bernstein (1922-). Because of this musical connection, the fight song is sometimes called "Step to the Rear."

THE NC-4
(University of South Carolina)

When the University of South Carolina first adopted a fight song in the 1930s, it chose the wordless trio or main melody of "The NC-4" or "The NC-4 March" (1919), the second best-known piece by Frederick Ellsworth Bigelow (1873-1929). "NC-4" has reportedly also been used by the University of Kansas and at California State University, Chico, for their "Fight Song." Bigelow's best-known composition is the famous "Our Director" or "Our Director March" (1895), whose outstanding strains have been used as a fight song ("Our Director") at Harvard University, as an alma mater ("Rice's Honor") at Rice University, and as another fight song ("Hail the White and Purple") at Furman University. Like "NC-4," the U.S. Navy airplane which first crossed the Atlantic Ocean, Bigelow's relatively few compositions certainly have traveled far.

CLEAR THE WAY FOR USC
(University of Southern California)

Still-remembered, "Clear the Way for USC" is an early college delight written around 1903 by P. S. Shanahan, class of 1904. Note that the genders are given equal status. Shanahan also wrote another energetic sports song, "Who We Are," at about the same time.

MARCHING SONG OF USC
(University of Southern California)

"Marching Song of USC," by Lois Oxnam, features a short verse and a much longer chorus. Probably written in the early twentieth century, when none of the songs of the University of Southern California used the term "Trojan," it is one of the earliest sports songs of the Los Angeles school. By 1929, the term "Trojan" appears in USC songs.

USC, BELOVED 'VARSITY
(University of Southern California)

Lois Ely, class of 1914, won first prize in a circa 1913 song contest for this vigorous and enthusiastic sports song. Much additional musical energy in the pre–World War I period was supplied by "USC Is Marching On!" and "Glory, Southern California," both of which used the tune from "Battle Hymn of the Republic," "USC Battle," which used the tune from "Maryland, My Maryland," and "Victory Song," which used the tune from "Our Director."

FIGHT FOR OUR DEAR OLD "T" "U"
(University of Toledo)

Written when the University of Toledo was known as the University of the City of Toledo, "Fight for Our Dear Old 'T'‘U'" was copyrighted in 1922. Its creator was C. J. Dyer, who is otherwise unknown. The song apparently is seldom used today. Another song with "Dear Old" in its title is "Dear Old Nebraska U," also known as "There Is No Place Like Nebraska." Actually the alma mater of the "Cornhuskers" of the University of Nebraska, Lincoln, this superior 1935 composition, created by Harry Pecha, has been in effect often treated as a fight song.

VERMONT VICTORIOUS
(University of Vermont)

Although no longer used by the "Catamounts" of the University of Vermont in Burlington, "Vermont Victorious" (sometimes spelled "Vermont Victorius") was written for the university by three students. A. F. Furman, class of 1919, H. P. Sharples, class of 1921, and L. F. Killick, class of 1922, published the song in 1918. The song was still at least somewhat active on the campus in the 1960s, when Eric Mortensen, class of 1966, submitted to the university a revision of the outdated World War I–era lyrics.

BEHOLD THE TEAM
(University of Virginia)

Created in the very early years of the twentieth century or the last years of the nineteenth, anonymous "Behold the Team" is an old-fashioned spirited song of athletic rivalry. Note that the schools with which Virginia was competing around the turn of the century were institutions such as Lafayette College, Lehigh University, and Yale University, all three of which are decidedly smaller in enrollment today than is the University of Virginia.

GLORY TO VIRGINIA
(University of Virginia)

When you see the word "Glory" at the beginning of a college fight song, there's a good chance that the tune used is the one from the immortal "Battle Hymn of the Republic." The rousing anonymous 1857 melody has been attached to the University of Georgia's "Glory, Glory, to Old Georgia," the University of Colorado's "Glory, Glory, Colorado," Auburn University's "Glory to Ole Auburn," and the University of Virginia's "Glory to Virginia." The lyrics for the last-mentioned song were written by "W. A., '05." It is quite likely that "W. A." is actually A. Frederick Wilson, class of 1905, who wrote other songs for the Charlottesville school, and edited the 1906 collection, *Songs of the University of Virginia*.

HAIL THE ORANGE AND THE BLUE
(University of Virginia)

More or less of a fight song, "Hail the Orange and the Blue" is a gentler turn-of-the-century predecessor to the strident "in your face" style of late twentieth-century sports competition. The tune is anonymous, but the words are by A. Frederick Wilson, class of 1905, who created several University of Virginia compositions.

VIRGINIA'S CAVALIER SONG
(University of Virginia)

Fulton Lewis Jr. (1903-1966), a well-known radio news personality around mid-century, wrote the music for "Virginia's Cavalier Song" or "The Cavalier Song" in 1923. Lewis was a 1925 graduate and Lawrence Haywood Lee Jr., the lyricist, was a 1924 graduate. The song, although not highly popular, is still reportedly heard on the campus in Charlottesville.

BOW DOWN TO WASHINGTON
(University of Washington)

Many other college songs have to artistically bow down to "Bow Down to Washington," the official fight song of the "Huskies" of the University of Washington. The creator of this superior composition was Lester J. Wilson, class of 1913. "Bow Down" was copyrighted in 1916.

YOH WASHINGTON
(University of Washington)

"Yoh Washington," apparently meaning "Yo Washington," was written by Robert Stevenson, a 1924 graduate of the University of Washington in Seattle, and was copyrighted in 1924. Stevenson seems to be the same person who published *Coronation Concerto,* for organ, and *A Manhattan Sonata,* for piano, both in 1954.

WISCONSIN SPIRIT
(University of Wisconsin at Madison)

Preceding by about two or three years the celebrated "On, Wisconsin" (1909), lyrics by Carl Beck, music by William Thomas

Purdy, "Wisconsin Spirit" was once popular with the "Badgers" of the University of Wisconsin at Madison. Frank L. Waller, class of 1907, who wrote both the words and the music, probably created this piece around 1906 or 1907. Waller was later involved with a number of other songs from the 1910s to the 1930s, usually supplying the melody.

COW BOY JOE
(University of Wyoming)

Lively "Cow Boy Joe," usually spelled "Cowboy Joe," is a fitting fight song for the "Cowboys" of the University of Wyoming in Laramie. It is a slightly modified version of the 1912 popular standard "Ragtime Cowboy Joe," by lyricist Grant Clarke (1891-1931) and composers Lewis F. Muir (1884-1950) and Maurice Abrahams (1883-1931). The piece was probably adopted by the university in the 1920s.

CHEER FOR THE GOLD AND BLACK
(Vanderbilt University)

Anonymous "Cheer for the Gold and Black" was copyrighted in 1911. It was apparently used for at least two decades by the "Commodores" of Vanderbilt University in Nashville, Tennessee.

TECH TRIUMPH
(Virginia Polytechnic Institute and State University)

From the title of this official fight song, it is apparent that the popular shortening of this institution's name to "Virginia Tech" goes back at least eighty years. The same is true of the sports nickname at Blacksburg, the "Hokies," as indicated in the chorus. ("Gobblers" is another nickname.) Copyrighted in 1919, this spirited march was created by Mattie E. Boggs and W. P. Maddux. In some sources, Boggs is erroneously referred to as "Goss."

FIGHT! FIGHT! BLUE AND WHITE
(Washington and Lee University)

Much less famous than the same school's "Washington and Lee Swing," by Mark W. Sheafe, Thornton Whitney Allen, and Clarence A. "Tod" Robbins, published in 1910, is "Fight! Fight! Blue and White." John Alexander Graham (1895-), class of 1914, wrote the melody and Carl E. L. Gill, class of 1921, wrote the lyrics, for their Lexington, Virginia, alma mater. Graham also wrote *Madrigals, Carols, and Folk Tunes,* a 1932 set of original Christmas music and arrangements for chorus, and the music for two 1938 songs, "A Child's Song of Christmas" (lyrics, Marjorie L. C. Pickthall) and "A Christmas Folk-Song" (lyrics, Lizette Woodworth Reese).

THE FIGHT SONG
(Washington State University)

The fight song of the "Cougars" of Washington State University in Pullman, that is, the still proudly played official sports song, is aptly titled "The Fight Song." Two music students, lyricist Zella Melcher, class of 1919, and composer Phyllis E. Sayles, class of 1922, collaborated on the piece in 1919. Melcher (1897?-1938) is also known by the name Zella Melcher McMicken, and Sayles (1897?-1971) is also known as Phyllis Sayles Davis. Sayles attended Northwestern University prior to going to Washington State, and in 1917 demonstrated her interest in college songs by arranging the 1917 edition of the *Northwestern University Song Book.* A number of other fight songs have been created for the school, for example, "Washington, My Glory" (1913), by James DeForest Cline (1885-1952) and "Cougar Conquest" (1960), by Paul Yoder (1908-1990), both by very notable band composers. Yet "The Fight Song" remains the preferred song, as demonstrated by its performance several times at the 1998 Rose Bowl game.

HAIL, WEST VIRGINIA
(West Virginia University)

The "Mountaineers" of West Virginia University use "Hail, West Virginia" (1915) as their fight song. While that fact is as clear as some mornings in the West Virginia hills, the authorship of the piece is as foggy as some mornings in the same locale. Earl Miller definitely wrote the melody and Ed McWhorter definitely was a collaborator, but historical sources are inconsistent as to precise authorship details. One version suggests that Miller and McWhorter collaborated on both words and music, another suggests that Miller wrote the music and McWhorter wrote the words, and yet another states that Miller and McWhorter wrote the music and Fred B. Deem wrote the lyrics. (Despite the greater detail of the last version, there is some reason to believe that Miller was the only composer and therefore his collaborator McWhorter had to have written the lyrics, perhaps with Deem.) However, no matter what the exact truth may be, the rousing march has been a favorite in Morgantown for many years.

BINGO, ELI YALE
(Yale University)

"Bingo, Eli Yale," also known as "Bingo, That's the Lingo," is a smooth, lively, and affable gem by one of the most famous Yale graduates, the great Broadway composer Cole Porter (1891-1964), class of 1913. It has been adapted by various high schools and other institutions. Porter wrote "Bingo" in 1910, and "Bull-Dog," a goofy but enduring college piece, in 1911.

BULL-DOG
(Yale University)

Although on the silly side, "Bull-Dog," also known as "The Bull Dog" and "Bull Dog! Bull Dog! Bow, Wow, Wow," has been as tough at surviving as its canine counterpart. Cole Porter (1891-1964), the legendary creator of musicals, wrote this piece in 1911 two years before his graduation from Yale University in 1913, and one year after his finer sports composition "Bingo, Eli Yale" (1910).

DOWN THE FIELD
(Yale University)

Stanleigh P. Friedman (1884-1960), class of 1905, wrote the extraordinary melody for "Down the Field" in 1904. Caleb W. O'Connor, class of 1904, wrote the lyrics for this official fight song of the "Bulldogs" of Yale University. Friedman later became a lawyer and notable composer, and two years later O'Connor wrote the words and music for "Cheer Pennsylvania," a fight song for the University of Pennsylvania. The smooth yet strongly transporting tune of "Down the Field," also known as "March on Down the Field," has been borrowed by many high schools and colleges, including the University of Tennessee, which performs it frequently, and the University of Oregon.

GLORY FOR YALE
(Yale University)

This march and one-step was most likely written around 1916, although not published until 1920. It is perhaps the second best-known song by Stanleigh P. Friedman (1884-1960), class of 1905, who created this melody along with the famous melody of "Down the Field" (1904). The lyrics are by Julian Arnold, class of 1917. A striking piece, it was still heard in the Yale Bowl in the 1950s.

WHOOP IT UP
(Yale University)

Stanleigh P. Friedman (1884-1960), Yale University class of 1905, apparently loved marches. In 1904 he composed the placid yet powerful march melody for his famous and much-borrowed classic, "Down the Field." (The lyrics were by Caleb W. O'Connor, class of 1904.) Two years later he whooped it up with "Whoop It Up," a march and two-step. The lyrics for this 1906 composition were by H. G. Dodge. Then, probably around 1916, he wrote a march and one-step called "Glory to Yale," words by Julian Arnold, class of 1917. Therefore, Friedman went from calm to wild to the heights of glory in a little over a decade.

SONG TEXTS
*(Arranged Alphabetically
by the Name of the College
or University)*

Allegheny Pep Song
(Allegheny College)

Briskly

Fair Al - ma Ma - ter, you've been true; Through thick or thin we'll
Join our song for the Blue and Gold; Up - hold our stand - ard

stick by you. You have been our shield; We will nev - er yield
as of old. Show them on the floor, How we make a score.

On the floor or field, And we're goin' to start to
Ev - 'ry bo - y ROAR, For we're goin' to start to

45

Fight, Al - le - ghen - y Fight! Fight! Fight! Fight Al - le - ghe, with
Fight, Al - le - ghen - y Fight! Fight! Fight! Fight Al - le - ghe, with

all your might! It is up to you to pro -
all your might! It is up to you to pro -

tect the Gold and Blue, Fight on to Vic - to - ry!
tect the Gold and Blue, Fight on to Vic - to - ry!

Cheer for Old Amherst
(Amherst University)

Come and sing, all ye loy - al Am - herst men, Come and
Soon our foe shall our strength in con - flict know, Soon our

give a rous - ing cheer, Join our line as we
pow - er they shall feel, Van - quished then they'll give

march a - long so fine, With hearts that have no fear.
way to Am - herst men, Whose cords are strong as steel.

Come primo

Cheer for old Am - herst Am - herst must win,_____ Fight to the fin - ish, Nev - er give in,_____ ish,

Glory, Glory to Old Amherst
(Amherst College)

Here's to old Am-herst, boys, a brim-ming glass of wine,
Hail to old Am-herst, boys, and give a lust-y cheer,

Here's to old Am-herst, boys, and days of Auld Lang Syne, Let
Cheer for old Am-herst, boys, the name we hold so dear,

ev-'ry Sen-ior, Jun-ior, Soph, and Fresh-man fall in line, While
Cheer for old Am-herst, boys, we'll make old Plu-to hear, While

we   go   march - ing   on.
we   go   march - ing   on.

Chorus

Glo - ry, glo - ry to old Am - herst, Glo - ry, glo - ry to old

Am - herst, Glo - ry, glo - ry to old Am - herst, As

Glory to Ole Auburn
(Auburn University)

For Boston
(Boston College)

56

here men are men and their hearts are true And the
ev - er with the Right shall Thy sons be found Till

tow - ers on the Heights reach to Heav'ns own blue. For
time shall be no more, and Thy work is crown'd! For

Bos - ton, for Bos - ton, Till the ech - oes ring a - gain!
Bos - ton, for Bos - ton, For Thee and Thine a - lone!

The Brown Cheering Song
(Boston University)

When Bru-
no - nia's Big Brown Team is in the game, And the

whole line is fight-ing to guard her name, And the

Bear growls like thun-der as the backs crash by, There's a

kill-ing on the old Hill to - night. Bru - no - nia's

ban - ners are wav - ing In tri - umph

on the hill; Bru - no - nia's co - horts are cheer - ing, For the Bear has made his kill, Yea! Yea! This day is Brown, Brown for -

ev - er, Let the van - quished count the

cost!_____ Then rise, rise and cheer,

boys, Till the last white line is crossed._____

Ever True to Brown
(Brown University)

We are ev-er true to Brown____ For we love our col-lege dear,____ And wher-ev-er we may

go,_____ We are read - y with a

cheer,_____ And the peo - ple al - ways

say_____ That you can't out - shine Brown

men_____ with their Rah! Rah! Rah! and their

Ki! Yi! Yi! And their B - R - O - doub - le U -

N_____ For we are N_____

Fight Song
(Clemson University)

The Big Red Team
(Cornell University)

See them plung - ing down to the goal, See the
Where the tow - ers rise o'er the lake, There our

rud - dy ban - ners stream, Hear the crash - ing ech - oes
fires in the night shall gleam, And the i - vied walls shall

Public Domain

roll,
quake,
As we cheer for the big red team. Yea! Yea! Yea!

Refrain

Cheer till the sound wakes the blue hills a - round, Make the

scream of the north wind yield To the

strength of the yell from the men of Cor - nell, When the

big red team takes the field, Yea! Yea! Three

thou - sand strong we march, march a - long, From our

home on the gray rock height, Oh! the

vic - t'ry is sealed when the team takes the field, And we

cheer for the red and white.

Fight for Cornell
(Cornell University)

From rock-y height,_____ we come to fight,_____ For the

name Cor - nell has made,_____ And we can

cheer,_____ with - out a fear,_____ That her good name will

ev - er fade._____ Fight to the end,_____ don't break or

bend,_____ Un - til our team has won the game,_____

And fight for might, for right, for Cor - nell's name,__

For the glo - ry that brings us fame.

Make all ad - van - ces, strong and sure to -

day,_____ Take all the chan - ces,

fate throws in the way, Fight

for the glo - ry, that is earned so well;

Vic - to - ry makes his - to - ry, So

fight for Cor - nell.

nell.

As the Backs Go Tearing By
(Dartmouth College)

As the backs go tear-ing by On the way to do or die, Ma-ny sighs and ma-ny tears, Min-gle with the Har-vard cheers, As the backs go tear-ing by, Mak-ing

gain on stead-y gain, Ech-o swells the sweet re-

frain, Dart-mouth's going to win to - day, Dart-mouth

sure must win to-day As the backs go tear-ing by.

Duke Blue and White
(Duke University)

Duke we thy an-thems raise___ For all thy

prais - es un - told___ We'll sing

for the Blue and White___ Whose co - lors we un -

fold　　　　　Firm　　stands　her　　line　of　　blue

For they are　loy - al　through and　through_____

Fight - ing　with　the　spir - it　true　All　for　the　love　of

Fordham Ram
(Fordham University)

Trio

Hail! Men of Ford - ham, Hail! On to the

fray!_____ Once more our foes as - sail

In strong ar - ray;_____ Once more the

old Ma - roon Wave_____ on high; We'll

sing our bat - tle songs: We do,_____ or

die!_____ With a Ram, a Ram for loy - al -

ty! With a Ram, a Ram, for vic - to - ry! To the

fight, the fight, To win our lau - rels bright!

Hail! Men of Ford - ham, Hail! On
to the fray!_____ Once more our
foes as - sail In strong ar - ray;_____

Once more the old Ma - roon, Wave_____ on

high;_____ We'll sing our bat - tle song:_____

We do,_____ or die!_____

Hail the White and Purple
(Furman University)

Hail___ the White and Pur - ple, Float -

ing on high.___ Hear shouts of tri -

umph, E - cho through the sky.

Rolls____ the cheer - ing on - ward Hail full and

free,____ Vict - 'ry be now____

for Fur - man Un - i - ver - si - ty.

Sons of Georgetown
(Georgetown University)

1. Sons of George - town Al - ma Ma - ter, Surft Po - to - mac's
   love - ly daugh - ter, Ev - er watch - ing
   by the wa - ter, Smiles on us to - day.

   Now her child - ren gath - er 'round her, Lo, with gar - lands
   they have crown'd her, Rev - 'rent hands and
   fond en - wound her, With the Blue and Gray.

2. Throned on hills be - side the riv - er, George town sees it
   flow for - ev - er, Sees the rip - ples
   shine and shiv - er, Watch - ing night and day.

   And each ten - der breeze up spring - ing, Rar - est wood - land
   per - fumes bring - ing, All its folds to
   full - ness fling - ing, Flaunts the Blue and Gray.

Public Domain

93

Harvardiana
(Harvard University)

Tempo di Marcia

With Crim - son in tri - umph flash - ing_____ 'Mid the

strains of vic - to - ry,_____ Poor

E - li's hopes we are dash - ing_____ In - to

blue ob - scu - ri - ty_____ Re -

sist - less our team sweeps goal - ward,_____ With the

fu - ry of the blast_____ We'll

fight   for   the   name   of   Har - vard_____   Till   the

last   white   line   is   passed._____

Har - vard!_____   Har - vard!_____

Har - vard! Har - vard! HAR - VARD! With
Crim - son in tri - umph flash - ing,_____ 'Mid the
strains of vic - to - ry,_____ Poor

E - li's hopes we are dash - ing_____ In - to

blue ob - scu - ri - ty_____ Re -

sist - less our team sweeps goal - ward,_____ With the

fu - ry   of   the   blast_____   We'll

fight   for the   name   of   Har - vard_____   Till the

last   white   line   is   passed._____

Ten Thousand Men of Harvard
(Harvard University)

For years past____ the teams of Crim - son____ have won____ tri - umph af - ter tri - umph from her foe,____ Her glo - ry____

For the loy - al sons of Har - vard know no fear._____ All rise_____ for Har - vard_____ And we'll

Football Song
(Haverford College)

safe-ty, The   grid-iron serves you   board,   For   one   and   all   can
shak-en   A - gainst op-po-nents'   plays,   With   one   ac - cord   for

play   foot - ball   Out   there   at   Hav - er   -   ford.
Hav - er - ford   A   song   of   vic - t'ry   raise.

Chorus

Hur -   rah   for   the   team   of   the   Scar - let   and

Black, For they have the skill and the know -

ledge, Straight down the field till the touch - down is

made, A score for our good old col - lege.

Indiana Fight!
(Indiana University)

Fight for_____ the Cream and Crim - son,_____ Loy - al

sons of our old I. U._____

Fight for_____ your Al - ma Ma - ter_____

114

And the school you love so true.

Fight for_____ old In - di -

an - a_____ See her vic - tor - ies

safe - ly   through_____   Go!

I.   U.!   Fight!   Fight!   Fight!   For   the

glo - ry   of   old   I.   U._____

Fight for LSU
(Louisiana State University)

Like Knights of Old_____ Let's fight to

hold_____ The glo - ry of the Pur - ple

Gold._____ Let's car-ry through,_____ Let's die or

do_____ To win the game for dear old

L. S. U._____ Keep try-ing for_____ A high-er

score;_____ Come on and fight, we want some

more, some more. Come on you Ti - gers, Fight! Fight!

Fight! For Dear Old L. S. U!_____ Rah!

Lead - ing them to vic - to - ry!

Let's have a touch - down! Let's have a touch - down!

Ti - gers, Fight, Fight, Fight! Rah! Rah! Like Knights of

mf

D.S. al Fine

Sons of Marshall
(Marshall University)

Proud are we of the his - to - ry of a ver - y fam - ous man_____ They gave our Col - lege his

122

name be - cause that's the kind of a man he was.

Rev - o - lu - tion to Con - sti - tu - tion his

rise to fame be - gan_____ He was the third Chief

Proud - ly we wear our Col -

ors   Love   and   loy - al - ty   to

pledge_____   Sure   from   far   and   near   you

Oh! Didn't He Ramble
(New Mexico State University)

Bus - ter was the black sheep of the Bee - be fam - i -

ly,_____ They tried their best to break him of his

rough and row - dy ways,_____ At last they had to

get a Judge to give him nine - ty days, Oh! didn't he

Chorus

ram - ble ram - ble? He

ram - bled all a - round   in and out the

town, Oh didn't he ram - ble, ram -

ble. He ram - bled till the but - chers cut him

1. down. Oh didn't he 2. down.

Old New York University
(New York University)

Old New York Un - i - ver - si - ty,

charms a - way all ad - ver - si - ty,

Stead - y and true, we'll be to you,

132

Loy - al sons of N. Y. U. RAH RAH RAH Raise on high the vi - o - let, col - or we'll ne'er for -

Oberlin Pep Song
(Oberlin College)

stand - ard,   In   what e'er   we
loy - al,   In   our love   for

do._____   "Hail,   hail,   the
thee._____

gang's   all   here!"   Round   thy   col - ors

old;_____ We'll stick to -

gether For the Crim - son_____ and

1.

2.

Gold._____

Gold._____

The Buckeye Battle Cry
(Ohio State University)

In Old Co - lum - bus there's a team, that's known through - out the land; E - lev - en war - riors

138

brave and bold whose fame will ev - er stand, And

when the ball goes o - ver, our cheers will reach the

sky, O - hi - o field will hear a - gain the

Buck - eye bat - tle cry._____

Chorus

Drive! Drive on down the field_____

Men of the scar - let and gray_____

cheer you as we go_____ Our

hon - or de - fend, so we'll fight to the

end for O - hi - o._____

Ohio State
(Ohio State University)

hi - o May a - ges pass E're de -
hi - o No mor - tal hand can ef -

feat shall mar thy pride May vict - 'ry for a
face our faith in thee We know thine ev - er -

thou - sand years up - on thy ban - ners ride
last - ing name will stand through e - tern - i - ty

O - hi - o's fame in the

field and game is a joy to all the thou - sands who sup -

port her name Hear the cry "Hold 'em State" Nev - er

die Nev - er wait The fight - ing blood is in our ev - ry

vein Rah! Rah! Our her - oes fight for O -

hi - o's right When the whis - tle blows they're read - y for their

fate With Car - mens call our

foes will fall three cheers for O - hi - o

State. Rah! Rah! O - State.

Rally, Ohio!
(Ohio State University)

Ral - ly, O - hi - o, ral - ly a - gain, And we'll

Public Domain

fol - low our team to vic - t'ry. Shout - ing and

plead - ing, de - mand - ing, en - treat - ing, We're send - ing our

yells to the sky! Sh! Boom! Rah! E - yah, O -

hi - o,   And   "fight, boys,   let's   fight."   Stand   by   the

team   with   all   your   might.____   Tramp,   tramp,   tramp,   the   boys   are

march - ing;   Ral - ly   once   more   and   we're   sure   of   vic - to -

Fight On, State
(Pennsylvania State University)

Fight on, State,___ Fight on, State,___

152

Strike your gait____ and win;____

Vic - to - ry____ we__ pre - dict for thee,__

We're ev - er true____ to you

dear   old   White____   and   Blue.   On - ward, State,_

On - ward,   State,___   Roar,

Li - ons,   roar;_____   We'll   hit   that   line,   roll

up the score, fight on to vic - tory ev - er, more, Fight

on, on, on, on, on, Fight

on, on, Penn State!

The Nittany Lion
(Pennsylvania State University)

Ev - er - y col - lege
There's_ old Pitts - burgh

has a le - gend____ Passed__ on from
with its Panth - er_____ And__ Penn her

Public Domain

156

hon - ored   i - dols_____   There's but   one   that
with   its   Ti - ger_____   And____   Cor - nell

stands   the   test_____   It's the   State - ly
with   its   Bear_____   But__   speak - ing

Nitt - a - ny   Li - on_____   The   sym - bol
now__   of   vic - t'ry_____   We'll   get   the

of   our   best._____
Li - on's   share._____

poco rit.

Chorus

Hail   to   the   Li - on_____

a tempo

Loy - al   and   true_____

Hail,   Al - ma Ma - ter,_____

with   your   white   and   blue_____

Penn   State   for - ev - er_____

mol - der of men and wo - men

Fight for her hon - or_____ and

vic - to - ry a - gain._____

Victory
(Pennsylvania State University)

fray_____ Wheth - er it be Pitt or Penn,

Har - vard or Cor - nell, Play the game ev -'ry

man And we will win a - gain.

Chorus

marcato

Fight, fight, fight, for the blue and white, Vic - to - ry will our slo - gan be, Dear Al - ma Ma - ter, Fair - est of all, Thy loy - al sons will o - bey thy call to fight, fight, fight, with

all their might, ev - er the goal to gain;

In - to the game for Penn State's fame Fight on to vic - to -

1.

ry._____

2.

ry._____

All a - long the line.

The Orange and the Black,
(Princeton University)

Al-though Yale has al - ways fav - ored The vi - o - let's dark
Thro' the four long years of col - lege, Midst the scenes we know so
When the cares of life o'er take us, Ming - ling fast our locks with

blue, And the gen - tle sons of Har - vard To the crim - son rose are
well, As the mys - tic charm to know - ledge We vain - ly seek to
grey, Should our dear - est hopes be - tray us, False for - tune falls a -

true, We will own the lil - lies slen - der, Nor hon - or shall they
spell; Or we win ath - let - ic vic - t'ries On the foot - ball field or
way, Still we'll ban - ish care and sad - ness As we turn our mem - 'ries

lack, While the Ti - ger stands de - fen - der Of the Or - ange and the
track, Still we work for dear old Prince - ton And the Or - ange and the
back, And re - call those days of glad - ness 'Neath the Or - ange and the

Black; We will own the lil - lies slen - der, Nor hon - or shall they
Black, Or we win ath - let - ic vic - t'ries On the foot - ball field or
Black; Still we'll ban - ish care and sad - ness As we turn our mem - 'ries

lack, While the Ti - ger stands de - fen - der Of the Or - ange and the Black.
track, Still we work for dear old Prince - ton And the Or - ange and the Black.
back, And re - call those days of glad - ness 'Neath the Or - ange and the Black.

The Princeton Cannon Song
(Princeton University)

In Prince - ton town we've got a team That knows the way to play,_____ With

Prince - ton spir - it back of them, They're sure to win the day_____ With cheers and song we'll ral - ly round The can - non as of yore,_____ And

Fight! fight! for ev - 'ry yard,_____ Prince - ton's

hon - or to de - fend. 'Rah! 'rah! 'rah! 'rah! Ti - ger!

Siss! Boom! ah!_____ And lo - co - mo - tives by the score,_____

For we'll fight with a vim, That is dead sure to

win For old Nas - sau._____

1.

2. *Fine*

sau,_____

Fine

Princeton Forward March
(Princeton University)

Come fall in line, we're all in line for Prince - ton, To show we're true_____ to team or

crew._____ We'll march a - long with cheer and song for

Prince - ton,   To show we're   loy - al   through   and

through._____   Read - y,   Nas - sau Hall,   hear   the

cresc.

battle call: "Prince - ton, for - ward march."

Refrain Marziale ben marcato

Prince - ton for - ward march to vic - to - ry, Prince - ton, lead the

way. Prince - ton, for - ward march to vic - to - ry, This is the Ti - ger's

day.   Yea!   Prince - ton,   for - ward march to   vic - to - ry,

fz

Fight   with   brain   and   brawn.   We'll   leave   old   E - li
                                                        Har - vard
                                                        Dart - mouth

trail - ing   in   the dust,   As   we   go march - ing   on.   on.

Princeton Jungle March
(Princeton University)

'Way down in old New Jer - sey, In that far - off jun - gle land, There lives a Prince - ton

Ti - ger, Who will eat right off your hand. But

when he gets in bat - tle With the oth - er beasts of

prey, He fright - ens them al - most to death, In

this pe - cul - liar way: Wow, wow,

wow - wow - wow, Hear the Ti - ger roar;

Wow, wow, wow - wow - wow, Roll - ing up a

Ramble Song
(Princeton University)

Prince - ton has a Ti - ger With
The Ti - ger plays at foot - ball With

long and shag - gy hair;_____ And E - li has a
vig - or, force and vim,_____ And in the game of

bull - dog: They are a dan - dy pair____ When these two get to -
base - ball Old Yale is pie for him,____ The fa - mous E - li

geth - er To have a lit - tle scrap,____ Just
bull - dog Will soon be in the soup,____ A -

watch the Ti - ger swift - ly push The bull - dog off the
gain we'll see the Ti - ger make The bull - dog loop the

ram - - - ble,____ ram - - -

ble, The way we'll beat Old E - li will be

fine. 'Rah! 'Rah! And then he will fine.

Hail, Purdue
(Purdue University)

To your call once more we ral - ly, Al - ma
When in aft - er years we're turn - ing, Al - ma

187

Ma - ter, hear our praise;_____
Ma - ter, back to you,_____

Where the Wa - bash spreads its val - ley, Filled with
May our hearts with love be yearn - ing, For the

Joy our voi - ces raise._____
scenes of old Pur - due._____

From the skies in swell - ing ech - oes Come the
Back a - mong your path - ways wind - ing Let us

cheers that tell the tale,_____ Of your
seek what lies be - fore,_____ Fond - est

vict - 'ries and your he - roes, Hail Pur - due! We
hopes and aims e'er find - ing, While we sing of

Hail, Hail to old Pur - due! Our

friend - ship may she nev - er lack,_____

Ev - er grate - ful ev - er true, Thus we

raise   our   song   a - new,_____

Of   the   days   we've   spent   with   you,   All

hail   our   own   Pur - due._____   due._____

Come Join the Band
(Stanford University)

wav - ing   ov - er - head._____
field we'll force our way,_____

Stan - ford for you,_____   Each loy - al
And   on   the   green_____   Each man who

com - rade brave and true_____
joins   the   ser - pen - tine_____

With might and main sings
With might and main sings

this re - frain, "For - ev - er and for -
this re - frain, "For - ev - er and for -

ev - er Stan - ford red."
ev - er Stan - ford red."

Down, Down the Field
(Syracuse University)

Down, down the field goes old Syr - a - cuse! Just see those backs hit the line and go through._____

Down, down the field they go march - ing, fight - ing for the
Or - ange staunch and true. Rah! Rah! Rah! Vic - t'rys in
sight for old Syr - a - cuse, each loy - al son knows she
that

ne'er more will lose,_____ for we'll fight, yes, we'll
Col - gate

fight, and with all our might, for the glo - ry of

old Syr - a - cuse. Rah! Rah! Rah! cuse._____

The Saltine Warrior
(Syracuse University)

In the / On the

days of old when the knights were bold, Ev' - ry
bat - tle field, he will nev - er yield; Oth - er

cit - y had its war - ri - or man,_____ In the days of
war - riors of the world he's there to meet._____ As the years roll

204

new when the fights are few, You will view them from a
past, he fights till the last, And he nev - er yet has

big grand - stand._____ In our col - lege town one has
known de - feat._____ To lay low his pride oth - er

great re - nown, If the game of foot - ball he should
knights have tried, But this war - rior they have grown to

play._____ With his pig - skin ball he is cheer'd by
fear._____ When the day is done and the vic - try's

all, He's the Sal - tine War - rior of to - day.
won, You will hear his prais - es loud and clear.

Sal - tine War - rior is a bold, bad man, And his wea - pon is a

pig - skin ball._____ When on the field he takes a
good firm stand, He's the he - ro of large and small._____
He will rush towards the goal with might and main; His op -

po - nents all fight but they fight in vain, Be - cause the

Sal - tine War - rior is a bold, bad man, And is

vic - to - ri - ous o - ver all. all.

The Aggie War Hymn
(Texas A&M University)

Hull - a - bal -oo! Can -eck! Can -eck! Hull -a - bal -oo! Can -eck! Can -eck!

All hail! to dear old Tex - as A and
Good - bye to Tex - as U - ni - ver - si -

M_____ Ral - ly a - round Mar - oon and
ty,_____ So long to the Or - ange and the

White;_____ Good - luck to the
White;_____ Good - luck to the

dear old Tex - as Ag - gies,
dear old Tex - as Ag - gies,

They are the boys who show the fight._____
They are the boys who show the fight._____

That good old Ag - gie spir - it thrills_____
"The eyes of Tex - as are up - on_____

us
you,"
And makes us yell and yell and
That is the song they sing so

yell;_____
well;_____
So let's fight for
So good - bye to

dear old Tex - as A and M_____
Tex - as U - ni - ver - si - ty,_____

We're   goin'   to   beat   you   all   to
We're   goin'   to   beat   you   all   to

Chig - gar - roo - gar - rem!   Chig - gar - roo - gar - rem!
Chig - gar - roo - gar - rem!   Chig - gar - roo - gar - rem!

Rough! Tough! Real   Stuff!   Tex - as   A   and   M.
Rough! Tough! Real   Stuff!   Tex - as   A   and   M.

Brown and Blue Forever
(Tufts University)

'Tis Brown and Blue for - ev - er, men! Hur - rah for Tufts!

Tufts men are march - ing in - to the fight,
Tufts men, u - ni - ted, ev - er have won;

mf

Strong is our cour - age, our hearts are light.
Now play to - geth - er, we've just be - gun.

We'll win the game, boys, Cheer - ing for you,
Off with the ball, boys, fol - low the cry;

We'll shout for dear old Tufts.
"Slide home for dear old Tufts."

Put ev - 'ry man out, don't let them steal; Ral - ly now for
Get ev - 'ry lin - er, play safe and sure; Stead - y, boys, and

one   last   score!_____   Fill   all   those   ba-ses up   and
get   that   ball._____   Cheer   for   the   team a-gain   as

watch that   ball.   Tufts men   tear   home   while   spir - its   soar._____
Tufts speeds   on.   Cha -pel!   Re - ech - o   wide   the   call!_____

Ring!   thou   voice   of   vict - 'ry,   ring_____

Tufts is bound to win to - day._____ Tufts For -
ev - er now in cho - rus sing; Hon - or the Hill for
aye!_____ When the din of bat - tles o'er,_____

Flash the word to yon - der height_____

Then the tri - umph bell shall peal once more,

"All is joy at Tufts to - night."_____

Semper Paratus
(United States Coast Guard Academy)

Tempo di Marcia

From Az - tec shore to Arc - tic zone, To Eu - rope and Far

219

East, The Flag is car - ried by our ships In times of war and peace; And nev - er have we struck it yet In spite of foe - men's might, Who cheered our crews and

cheered a-gain For show-ing how to fight. So here's the

Coast Guard March-ing Song,_____ We sing on

land or sea._____ Through surf and

storm and howl - ing gale, High shall our

pur - pose be._____ "Sem - per Pa -

ra - tus" is our guide,_____ Our fame, our

glo - ry, too,_____ To fight to

save or fight and die! Aye! Coast Guard, we

1. are for you!_____ **2.** you!_____

Yea, Alabama!
(University of Alabama)

Yea Al - a - ba - ma! Drown 'em Tide! Ev -'ry 'Ba - ma man's be - hind you; Hit your stride! Go teach the "Bull - dogs" to be - have. Send the "Yel - low Jack - ets" to a

wa - ter - y grave! And if a man starts to weak - en, That's a

shame: For 'Ba - ma's pluck and grit have writ her name in Crim - son

flame. Fight on! fight on! fight on men! "Re -

mem - ber   the Rose Bowl:" We'll win   then.

Roll   on   to vic -t'ry!   Hit   your stride!   You're

Dix - ie's foot - ball   pride, Crim - son Tide!

Fight! Wildcats! Fight!
(University of Arizona)

Moderato e marziale

Hail! Ar - i - zo - na Wild - cats! Fight - ing for old U.
Hail! Ar - i - zo - na Town - cats! Cheer - ing for old U.

A. A rag - ing team of Wild - cats,
A. A loy - al gang of Town - cats,

Chorus

day! Fight! Wild - cats! Fight for Ar - i - zo - na, We're with you
day!

ev - er staunch and true,___ This day we hail you and we

cheer you,___ They can't de - feat the Red and Blue.___ Cir - cle the
Drib - ble the

ends and crash thru   cen - ter,___   Hit hard and   gain   on   ev - 'ry
floor and shoot   a   bas - ket,___ Guard, pass, and score on   ev - 'ry

play
play   Fight!   Wild - cats!   Fight! Fight! Fight! We'll

win   to - day. Fight! Wild - cats!   day.

Razorback Pep Song
(University of Arkansas)

Lively march time

Here are the Ra - zor - backs, Pride of old Ark - an - sas,
Play - ing the game to win, Fight - ing for Ark - an - sas,

Nev - er in du - ty lax, read - y to fight! We have the win - ning team,
Now let the fun be - gin, {opponent's name} good - night!

See how our col - ors gleam, Al - ways they'll be su - preme, The red and white.

Big C
(University of California at Berkeley)

Big "C" means to fight and strive and win for Blue and Gold. Gold-en Bear is e-ver watch-ing;
Palms of glo-ry we will win For Al-ma Ma-ter true. Stan-ford's men will soon be rout-ed

Day by day he
By our daz - zling

prowls,   And   when he hears the tread   Of
"C,"   And   when we sur - pen - tine,   Their

low - ly Stan - ford red, From his   lair he fierce - ly
red   will turn   to green, In   our   hour of   vic - to -

1.
growls.   Gr -rr-rah, Gr-rr-rah, Gr-r, r-r-r, r-r-rah!

2.
ry.

California Indian Song
(University of California at Berkeley)

We are fight - ing Cal - i - for - ni - ans, for the Gold and
We are hot - foot af - ter Stan - ford, camp - ing on her

Blue woo, woo, woo, We are start-ing on the war-path
trail; woo, woo, woo, With our tom-a - hawk be - fore us

for a scalp or two. Our blood's up and
we can nev - er fail. Get - ting read - y

sim - ply boil - ing, what can Stan - ford do?
for the war dance, all our war - riors true;

We are start-ing on the war - path for a scalp or
We are put-ting on our war - paint, Roy - al Gold and

two. So
Blue. For

Chorus

We're goin' to scalp you,

Stan - ford, We're goin' to scalp you

blue_____ > We'll do   it   with   your

tom - a - hawk we   took   from

you;_____ > All 'round our belts we'll

hang them to show all our friends who's

dead;_____ We're goin' to carve some block -

heads, whose scalps are red.

Sons of California
(University of California at Berkeley)

The Stanford Jonah
(University of California at Berkeley)

242

gun, And there's mu - sic in the air;_____ When our team runs on the field Stan - ford knows her fate is sealed, For the Gold - en Bear has

left   his   lair._____   When the   yells   from   lust - y

throats   Start   to   get - ting   Stan - ford's   goat,   And the

root - ing   sec - tion   seems a   howl - ing   mob,_____   Then you

grab your hat and shout, You let folks know you're a -

bout, For you know that Stan - ford's Jo - nah's on the

job._____ So then it's up with the Blue and Gold,

Chorus

Down with the Red, Cal - i - for - nia's

out for a vic - to - ry. We'll drop our

bat - tle axe on Stan - ford's head, When we

meet her, our team will sure - ly beat her,

Down on the Stan - ford Farm there'll be no

sound, When our Os - ki rips through the

air.   Like our   friend Mis - ter   Jo - nah, Stan - ford's

team   will   be   found   In the   tum - my   of   the

1. Gold - en Bear._____ So then it's   **2.** Bear._____

Fight CU, Down the Field
(University of Colorado)

Fight C. U. down the field, C. U. must

win; Fight, fight for vic - to - ry

C. U. knows no de-feat, We'll roll up a might - y score, Nev - er give in, Shoul - der to shoul - der we will fight! fight! fight!

Glory, Glory, Colorado
(University of Colorado)

Col - o - o - ra - do Var - si - ty comes march - ing on the field,

Col - o - ra - do Var - si - ty comes march - ing on the field,

Col - o - ra - do Var - si - ty comes march - ing on the field, Col - o -

-ra-do's bound to win! Glo - ry, Glo-ry to Col - o - ra - do,

Glo - ry, Glo - ry to Col - o - ra - do; Glo - ry, Glo - ry to Col - o

-ra - do, Hur - rah for the sil - ver and the Gold!__

The Orange and Blue
(University of Florida)

Tempo di Marcia moderato

On, brave old Flor - i - da,_____ Just keep on march - ing on your way;_____ On, brave old

253

Flor - i - da, And we will cheer you on your play. Rah!

Rah! Rah! And as you march a - long,____ We'll sing our

vic - t'ry song a - new;_____ With all your

might Go on and Fight, 'Ga - tors, Fight! For Dix - ie's right - ly   proud of

Chorus

you._____   So give a   Cheer   for the   Orange and

Blue,   Wav - ing for - ev - er!   for - ev - er! Flag

of old Flor - i - da, May she droop nev - er!___ We'll sing a

song for the flag to - day, Cheer for the

team at play, On to the goal we'll fight our way For

Flor - i - da._____ We will hit their line just like a

crash of thun-der, We will tear their backs and ends a-sun-der! Flor-i-da!

Flor - i - da! Rah!_____ So give a da._____

Cheer Illini
(University of Illinois at Urbana-Champaign)

There's a sound in my ear, It's a cheer it's a
Can you hear that big band, See those stands, ev - 'ry

cheer and I hear it all the time,_____ It's from
man is sing - ing that grand name,_____ That's

men who are true To the or - ange and blue
spir - it you see That's loy - al - ty

Public Domain

258

Back - ing the Ili - ni (line/nine), It's not whom we
And win Il - li - ni fame, That's why they

meet, not vic - t'ry, de - feat, That real - ly
fight with glo - ri - ous might, That's why that

means so much to me,_____ But my heart throbs with joy as I
all I ask for mine,_____ Is to sing, hat in hand, to the

back Il - li - nois And that grand old var - si -
best in the land And to cheer that Illi - ni

Chorus

ty._____
(line/nine)._____   Then cheer that good old

Il - li - ni (line/nine), Spur it on to vic - to -

Illinois Loyalty
(University of Illinois at Urbana-Champaign)

We're loy - al to you, Il - li - nois,_____ We're
We're loy - al to you, Il - li - nois,_____ To the

"Or - ange and Blue," Il - li - nois,_____ We'll back you to
Or - ange and Blue, Il - li - nois,_____ Your ban - ner in

Public Domain

stand 'Gainst the best in the land, For we know you have
hand, Comes a right roy - al band, From the ends of the

sand, Il - li - nois, Rah! Rah! So pass out that
land, Il - li - nois. Tho' rest - less we

ball Il - li - nois,_____ We're back - ing you all Il - li-
roam, Il - li - nois,_____ Your cam - pus is home, Il - li-

nois;_____ Our team is our fame pro-tect-or,
nois;_____ Your arms are out-spread to greet us,

On! boys, for we ex-pect a vict-'ry from you, Il - li -
Shout-ing, your thous-ands meet us, "wel-come to old, Il - li -

nois!_____ Che - he! Che-ha! Che - ha - ha - ha!
nois!"_____

Che - he! Che - ha! Che - ha - ha - ha!

Il - li - nois! Il - li - nois! Il - li - nois!

R.H.

Fling out that dear old flag of Or - ange and Blue, Lead on your
Fling out that dear old flag of Or - ange and Blue, We come, your

sons and daugh - ters, fight - ing for you; Like men of old, on
sons and daugh - ters, hom - ing to you; Your iv - ied walls be -

gi - ants Plac - ing re - li - ance, Shout - ing de - fi - ance,
fore us, Elm arch - es o'er us, Wild ring your cho - rus,

Os-key-wow-wow! A - mid the broad green plains that nour - ish our
Os-key-wow-wow! To win you world wide fame, in ma - ny a

land, For hon-est La - bor and for Learn-ing we
land For hon-est La - bor and for Learn-ing we

stand, And un - to thee we pledge our heart and hand, Dear
stand, And home ward turn with loy - al heart and hand, Dear

Al - ma Ma - ter Il - li - nois.
Al - ma Ma - ter Il - li - nois.

I'm a Jayhawk
(University of Kansas)

Talk a - bout the soon - ers the Ag -gies and the braves, Talk a - bout the

ti - ger and his tail,_____ Talk a - bout the

husk - ers, those old corn - hus - kin' boys, But

I'm a bird to make 'em weep and wail._____

Chorus

'Cause I'm a jay, jay, jay, jay, jay - hawk up at Law - rence on the Kaw_____ 'Cause I'm a jay, jay, jay, jay, jay - hawk, With a

sis - boom hip hoo - rah._____

Got a bill that's big e - nough to twist the ti - ger's tail,

Husk some corn and lis - ten to the corn - husk - er's wail__

'Cause I'm a jay, jay, jay, jay,

jay - hawk, Rid - ing on a Kan - sas

1. gale._____ 'Cause I'm a

2. gale, and that's our team.____

Hail to U of L
(University of Louisville)

'Mid the shouts and cheer-ing of the throng,_____ Al - ma

Ma - ter hear our song_____ Let re - sound - ing

ech - oes   voi - ces   raise_____   Spread - ing   far   thy

fame   thy   praise_____   Ev - er   loy - al

faith - ful   ev - er   true_____   Thus   we   make   our   pledge   to

you_____ And we'll nev - er fail but we'll al - ways

hail U. of L. Hail to you! All hail!_____ All hail to

Chorus

Dear old U. of L._____ Hail to the Card - 'nal

p - f

and the Black_____ Thy sons and daugh - ters love thee

well_____ Their faith and love will ne'er grow slack_____

Deep in our hearts thy deeds thy name_____ And glor - ious

victo'ries shall remain_____ You'll always be our own real and true Kentucky home Hail to you Dear U. of L._____ All hail to

Maryland, My Maryland!
(University of Maryland)

Thou wilt not cow - er in the dust, Mar - y - land, My Mar - y - land! Thy beam - ing sword shall nev - er rust, Mar - y - land, My

Go! Tigers, Go!
(University of Memphis)

Go, Ti - gers, go;___ go on to vic - to - ry,

Be a win - ner through and through,_____

Fight, Ti - gers, fight 'cause we're go - ing all the way.

Fight Fight for the blue and gray and say let's

Go, Ti - gers, go!_____ go on to

vic - to - ry, See our col - ors bright and

true_____ It's Fight now with -

out a fear, Fight now let's shout a cheer,

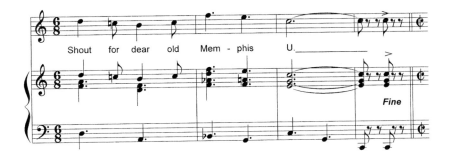

Shout for dear old Mem - phis U._____

Fine

Go, Tigers, go!

Go, Tigers, go!

Yea_____Tigers!

D.C. al Fine

tremolo

Varsity
(University of Michigan)

gan!_____ Var - si - ty,

Down the field, Nev - er yield, Raise high our

shield. March on to vic - to - ry for

you, Oh Var - si - ty!_____

a tempo

ty!_____ *vigoroso*

ff

Var - si - ty, Down the field, Nev - er yield, Raise high our shield. March on to vic - to - ry for Mich - i - gan, and the Maize and Blue Oh,

Win for Michigan
(University of Michigan)

March tempo

Mich - i - gan oh Mich - i - gan to us are dear Thy mem - o - ries and name, Thy sons of old true war - riors bold, Have fought and won thee fame. So we in fil - ial loy - al - ty Are

out to fight for thee And

by our might, to do and dare, bring vic - to - ry.

Refrain

Raise a might - y cheer for good old Mich - i - gan And

up and dar-ing force the line of bat - tle Drive back the

Foe and ne'er give way But fight, fight, fight, fight with all your might For we're

1. bound to win to - day. **2.** bound to win to - day.

Tiger Song of U of M
(University of Missouri at Columbia)

We've got your num - ber Kan - sas and we
It can't be did, it can't be did, You

know what you can do, We know just where your
heard us tell you so, We kicked that ball a

Public Domain

Jay   Hawk roosts   We   know   his   col - or
mile   a - way,   You   had   to   watch   it

too.   We'll   pull   the   feath - ers
go.   High   up   it   sailed,   and

from   his   tail   His   wings we'll stretch and
o'er   the   goal,   From   the bleach - ers came the

North Dakota U
(University of North Dakota)

We firm-ly stand pledged heart and hand A-gain our

voi - ces join in song_____ True

com - rades of the prair - ies, Our

faith is ev - er full and strong_____ When

thus we stand, pledged hand and hand, When

e'er our voi - ces rise_____ Where e'er our

he - roes strive, Where e'er our ban - ner flaunts the

skies_____ It's for You North Da - ko - ta

U_____ That we sing, your sons and daugh - ters

true_____ Cheer - ing our com - rades to vic - to - ry____

Re - new - ing al - le - gi - ance to U. N!

D! Your hon - or we up - hold in ev - 'ry con -

Fight, North Texas
(University of North Texas)

Lively

Let's give a cheer for North Tex - as State

Cheer for the Green and White_____ Vic - t'ry's in

store   but   what e're   the   score   Our   men   will

ev - er   fight,   fight,   fight,   fight   Shoul - der   to

shoul - der   they   march a - long   Men   with   a

Mighty Oregon
(University of Oregon)

She is small our Al - ma Ma - ter, But she rules with strength and
Ral - ly fel - lows, stand be - hind them, They are do - ing all they

right, What she lacks in mass and num - bers, She makes up for in her
can, Back the team in sun and shad - ow, Back the cap - tain, back each

fight, Or - e - gon is nev - er beat - en 'Till the fin - al whis - tles
man. They will car - ry home the vic - t'ry To old Dea - dy's hal - lowed

call, Who can tell her tale of tri - umph? Scores can nev - er show it
hall; Give the team the best that's in you, Give your Al - ma Ma - ter

Con Spirito

all. Or - e - gon, our Al - ma Ma - ter,
all.

p - f

We will guard thee on and on,_____ Fel - lows

gath - er round and cheer her,____ Chant her

glo - ry, Or - e - gon;_____ Roar the

prais - es of her war - riors, Sing the

Cheer Pennsylvania
(University of Pennsylvania)

Used by permission of the University of Pennsylvania Archives

Trio

Cheer,   Penn - syl - van - ia,   Cheer   ev - er -

more,_____   We're   here   to   see   the   Red   and

Blue   score   and   score;   And   when   we   give

a re - sound - ing Hoo - rah, Hoo -

rah,_____ Ev - er loy - al to old

cresc.

Penn - syl - va - ni - a._____

Fine

Fight On, Pennsylvania
(University of Pennsylvania)

O'er Penn - syl - van - ia's walls, With i - vy o - ver - grown, Our thoughts will ev - er lin - ger, The tend - 'rest we have known. We of - fer heart and

soul And give our all in praise; When men of Penn are fight - ing, This song to them we'll raise.

Chorus

Fight on! Penn - syl -

van - ia!   Put the   ball   a - cross   the

line,_____   Fight!   you   Penn - syl -

van - ians,   There   it   goes   a -

cross this time.

Red and Blue, we're with you, And we're

cheer - ing for your men;_____ Then

Fight!   Fight!   Fight!   Penn - syl - va - ni - a,

rit.

1.

Fight   on_____   for   PENN!

a tempo

2.

PENN!_____

The Pitt Panther
(University of Pittsburgh)

"Let's sing_____ the sto - ry_____ of

p - ff **Grandioso 2nd time**

Pitts - burgh's glo - ry,_____ The Old Pitt Pan - ther is o'er us_____ No foe can stand up be - fore us;_____ On field_____ or camp - us_____

We lead_____ the way,_____ We're

with you all to a man there___ Three cheers for the

1. Old Pitt Pan - ther."_____

2. Pan - ther."_____

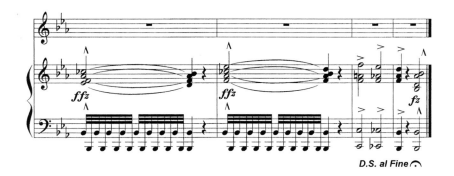

Pittsburgh's Big Team
(University of Pittsburgh)

Hark! Hark! Hark! to the noise and the roar, For the
Big Pitt Team is mov - ing, Watch them now pile up the
score; O - ver the goal line see them, Rah! Rah!

327

Sweep - ing   right on thru the foe,   On - ward in tri - umph they're

rov -   ing; For no line   can hold, Boys in Blue and Gold, When they're

Pitts - burgh's   Big   Team.   Team.

Rhode Island Cheer Song
(University of Rhode Island)

Allegro moderato

For old Rhode Is - land will win to - day   Oh look at her team

fight - ing all the way, Watch how they rip 'em left and right un - til they've crossed ev - 'ry chal - ky line of white, and while they're fight - ing for

vic - to - ry. We'll cheer for the white and blue,_____

Rise! Cheer a - gain Rhode Is - land State for - ev - er, and we'll

1.
win to day For old Rhode day._____
2.

Carolina Fight Song
(University of South Carolina)

Ca - ro - li - na Let your voi - ces ring To you we sing our prai - ses high_____ Ring out! Sing out! On to vic - to - ry For - ev - er fight we'll

Public Domain

332

do or die_____ Ca - ro - li - na

Fight with all your might Let all u - nite in proud a -

claim_____ Then Batt - tle on to - geth - er One and

all for - ev - er. Fight, we've got to win the game. Rah!

Rah! Rah! Gar - net and Black we raise,

Game - cocks for - ev - er praise, So Fight for

Ca - ro - li - na, Cheer for Car - o - li - na, Hail to our

1.,2. U. S. C.   3. Ca - ro - li -

na, We cheer for - ev - er U. S. C.____

Fight! USC
(University of South Carolina)

Fight! U. S. C._____ Go on to vic - to - ry_____ We'll
cheer for you, Fight for U. S. C._____ Our Team is best;
Stands the test, On - ward to glo - ry strong and tough, Ev - er true,
Game - cocks! Fight! Fight! So con - quer all_____ Don't let our
ban - ner fall____ Be - cause we're PROUD of U. S.
C._____ Our mot - to is FIGHT! Game - cocks! Fight
on for vic - to - ry U. S. C._____

The Fighting Gamecock Song
(University of South Carolina)

South Car - o - li - na, Let's ring the bell,

Let's ring the bell to - day._____

Used by permission of Buzz Purcell

337

Let's give 'em raz - zle, Let's give 'em daz - zle,

Give it to 'em all the way._____

Fight fight - ing Game - cocks, Let's show 'em how,

Let's show 'em how to win,_____ For we're

"C" - "A" - "R" - "O" - "L" - "I" - "N" - "A" right to the

1.
ver - y end.

2.
end._____

The Fighting Gamecocks
Lead the Way
(University of South Carolina)

Hey! Let's give a Cheer, Car - o - li - na is here The Fight - ing Game - cocks

THE FIGHTING GAMECOCKS LEAD THE WAY, Arranged by James Pritchard, words by Paul Dietzel, adapted from:
STEP TO THE REAR, by Carolyn Leigh and Elmer Bernstein
Copyright 1967 Carolyn Leigh and Elmer Bernstein   Copyright Renewed
All Rights Controlled and Administered by EMI Unart Catalog Inc.
WARNER BROS. PUBLICATIONS U.S. INC., Miami, FL 33014

340

That's   when   the   Cocks   get   go - ing.

Hail   to   our   col - ors   of   Gar - net   and   Black,

in   Car - o - li - na   pride   have

Let's give a cheer Car - o - li - na is here,

Go Fight - ing Game - cocks all the

way!_____ Hey! way!_____

The NC-4
(University of South Carolina)

Clear the Way for USC
(University of Southern California)

There's a col - lege in a sun - ny, south - ern land, And we love, yes, love it well; Ev -'ry year we gath - er there a hap - py band, For we love, yes, love it well; Ev' - ry

346

bod-y tips his hat to U. S. C. 'Tis our own dear col-lege

home: And we nev-er shall for-get old U. S. C. Where-so-

Chorus

ev-er we may roam.____ We are the boys of U. S.

high ring out the cry for U. S. C. Read-y all to shout the call for

U. S. C. Clear the way, pre-pare the fray, for

U. S. C. We are march-ing to vic - to - ry.____

Marching Song of USC
(University of Southern California)

'Mid south - ern skies a thou - sand strong, We march to the field to -
day, With cheer and song we march, march a - long To
cheer for the boys in the fray. Rah! Rah! Rah! Three long cheers for the

Chorus

var - si - ty, Var - si - ty of South - ern Cal - i -

forn - ia A wave of sound it e - choes a - round

Var - si - ty of South - ern Cal - i - forn - ia. We

swing, swing a - long, We sing, sing a - long, Like the breeze as it comes from the sea, And u - ni - ted we stand A strong - heart - ed band, The men of U. S. C.

USC, Beloved 'Varsity
(University of Southern California)

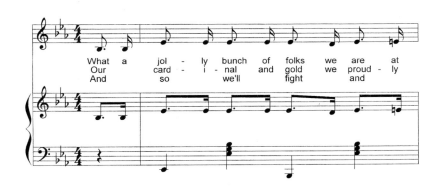

What a jol - ly bunch of folks we are at
Our card - i - nal and gold we proud - ly
And so we'll fight and

U. S. C. Hip hoo - ray! Hip hoo - rah! Hip hoo -
wave for thee, Oh, U. S. C. be - loved 'Vars - i -
yell and sing, Vic - to - ry, our be - loved 'Vars - i -

ree!　At our work and at our play we're al - ways
ty!　Our men, we cheer un - til they win the
ty!　We'll have her ri - vals scared, as scared as

true to thee, Oh, U. S. C. be - lov - ed 'Var - si -
vic - to - ry, Hip hoo - ray! Hip hoo - rah! Hip hoo -
they can be! Hip hoo - ray Hip hoo - rah! Hip hoo -

Chorus

ty!
ree!　Then let us yell! And let us
ree!

cheer! Un - til old Stan - ford quakes with

fear, Our team is grit - ty; They'll win the

vic - 'try! Oh, U. S. C. Rah! Rah! for thee.

Ritard.

Fight for Our Dear Old "T" "U"
(University of Toledo)

raise high the gold and blue a-bove you, Keep her stand-ards

ev - er a - mong the staunch and brave

High o'er our heads vic - to - rious Long may they ev - er wave! *(spoken)* Rah! Rah!

Vermont Victorious
(University of Vermont)

High o'er the wa - ters of lake Cham - plain
When the war trum - pet first called to arms

Now we re - main___ to up - hold the name of
Hin - den - burg's line___ which de - fied the world has

Ver - mont strong and true_____ So to
crum - pled 'neath our thrust_____ But the

keep all things we___ love at U. V. M. is
boys who fought in___ France while o - ver there is left

Ver - mont____ let's fight for Ver - mont_____ whose

sons have ne'er known fear. We will

tear up_____ our might - y ri - vals_____ and

pile   up   score   on   score   Come   boys   let's

fight   fight   fight   for   old   Ver - mont   for

Ver - mont   ev - er - more._____   Let's   fight   for

Behold the Team
(University of Virginia)

Be - hold the team of U. V - a, So heart - y and so hale; We've licked Lafa - yette and Le - high too And now we'll lick Old Yale! And now we'll lick Old Ya - a - ale! And

now   we'll   lick   Old   Yale!   We've   licked   Lafa - yette   and

Le - high   too,   And   now   we'll   lick   Old   Yale!   We've

licked   Lafa - yette   and   Le - high   too,   And   now   we'll   lick   Old   Yale!

Glory to Virginia
(University of Virginia)

we go march-ing on.
we go march-ing on.
we go march-ing on.   Glo - ry! glo-ry to Vir -

gin - ia!   Glo - ry! glo-ry to Vir - gin - ia!

Glo - ry! glo-ry to Vir-gin - ia! As we go march-ing on.

Hail the Orange and the Blue
(University of Virginia)

The ban - ner of old E - li's sons is
Then fill your glass - es to the brim and

bright and fair to see, And Prince - ton's ti - ger
raise them to the skies, And pledge each heart in

waves his tail in play - ful ec - sta - sy_____ Old
loy - al - ty, the ban - ner as she flies_____ We'll

ritard

Har - vard flaunts her crim - son flag, the
sing Vir - gin - ia's health and fame and

sun - set's gold - en hue,_____ But fair - er than these
roy - al friend - ships true,_____ And cheer, each moth - er's

flags, all hail the Or - ange and the Blue.
son of us, the Or - ange and the Blue.

Virginia's Cavalier Song
(University of Virginia)

March Time

Come and sing dear old Vir - gin - ia's name____ And____ make the Blue Ridge roar_____ For the world yields hon - or to her name____ Who___ knew her deeds of

yore   Then___ make each heart a flow - ing bowl__

And pour our pledg - es strong_____ As__

down the ag - es still we roll_____ Vir -

gin - ia's tri - umph song.

Once more our might has won the fight_____

We gain the vic - tor's due_____

And all men raise their voice to praise_____

The or - ange and the blue_____

So through the years, like Cav - a - liers_____

We'll shout Vir - gin - ia's name_____

It e'er shall be on land and sea A

sign_____ of might and fame._____

Bow Down to Washington
(University of Washington)

Bow down___ to Wash - ing - ton!___ Bow
Bow down___ to Wash - ing - ton!___ Bow

Used by permission of Paxwin Music Corp.

down___ to Wash - ing - ton!_____ From the dis -tant lands they send their
down___ to Wash - ing - ton!_____ Hard - y are the men who wear the

teams of great re - nown,____ But on the field of bat - tle they are
Pur -ple and the Gold____ Joy -ous -ly we wel -come you With -

tramp - led to the ground. We shall carve our name____ In the
in the van - quished fold. Bring the Gold - en Bear,____ From his

Hall of Fame__ To pre-serve the mem-o-ry of our de-vo-tion.__
might-y lair____ For we're goin' to hang his car-cass in the North-land.__

Chorus

Heav - en help the foes of Wash - ing - ton,_____ They're
Heav - en help the foes of Wash - ing - ton,_____ They're

tremb-ling at the feet of might-y Wash - ing - ton._____ The
tremb-ling at the feet of might-y Wash - ing - ton._____ The

boys are there with bells,___ Their fight-ing blood ex - cels,___ It's
boys are there with bells,___ Their fight-ing blood ex - cels,___ It's

hard - er to push them o - ver their line Than pass the Dar - da - nelles.___
hard - er to push them o - ver their line Than pass the Dar - da - nelles.___

Vic - to - ry the cry of Wash - ing - ton._____
Vic - to - ry the cry of Wash - ing - ton._____

Yoh Washington
(University of Washington)

vic - to - ry,_____ We've got the pep, We've got the

rep,   Yea   Broth - er,   Give em a

who   ran, a who rah,   Yoh_____ Wash - ing - ton.

Wisconsin Spirit
(University of Wisconsin at Madison)

383

po - nents yield. Our team will win____ the game For they're fight - ing for____ the fame of Wis - con - sin, Wis -

con - - sin Hur - rah for old Wis -

con - sin U - rah - rah Wis - con - sin

cham - pion of the west.

Cow Boy Joe
(University of Wyoming)

syn - co - pa - ted gait - ed and you ought to hear the met - er to the roar of his re - peat - er how they run (YES RUN) When they see him___ come be - cause the west - ern folks all

know   He's   a   high   fa - lut - in'   root - in'   toot - in'

son - of - a - gun   from   old   Wy - o - ming   rag - time   cow - boy!__

Oh!   You   cow - boy!___   Rag - time   cow - boy   Joe!____

Cheer for the Gold and Black
(Vanderbilt University)

Cheer for the Gold and Black

wav - ing for - ev - er,

389

Flag of the com - mo - do - res
May it droop never We'll sing a
song for that flag to - day,

Tech Triumph
(Virginia Polytechnic Institute
and State University)

Tech - men, we're Tech - men, with spir - it true and faith - ful,
Fight men, Oh, fight men! we're go - ing to be cham - pions,

Back - ing up our team with hopes un - dy - ing;
Add - ing to our list an - oth - er vic - t'ry;

Tech - men, Oh, Tech - men, we're out to win to - day,
Foot - ball or base - ball, the games in which we star,

Show - ing "pep" and life with which we're try - ing;
They're the sports that made old V. P. fa - mous.

V. P.   old   V. P.   You   know   our hearts are   with   you,
Hold them,   just hold them!   You   know   the corp's be - hind   you,

In   our   luck which nev - er seems to   die;___
Watch - ing ev - 'ry move - ment that   you   make;___

Win   or lose we'll greet you with a   glad   re - turn - ing,
Win - ning games was noth - ing for our   teams be - fore us,

You're the pride of V. P. I. _____
Keep the "rep" for V. P.'s sake. _____

Chorus

Just watch our men so big and ac - tive,

mf *f*

Sup - port the O - range and Ma - roon, Let's go, Techs!

we know our ends and backs are strong - er,

With win - ning hopes, we fear de - feat no long - er,

To see our team plow thru the line, boys, De - term - ined

now to win or die;_____ So give a Ho - kie,

Ho - kie, Ho - kie, Hi!_____ Rae, Ri, old

V. P. I._____ I._____

Fight! Fight! Blue and White
(Washington and Lee University)

Hail to our Al - ma Ma - ter Hail to Vir - gin - ia's pride Boast of the old do - min - ion, Trust - ed, true and tried, Hail to her name so

glo - rious   Hail   to   the   White   and

Blue.   Hail   to   her   teams   vic -

to - rious   All   hail   our   W.   and   L.

U.   Then on for   Wash - ing - ton   and

Lee   Our mot - to,   Death   or   Vic - to -

ry   And wave the   Blue   and   White   on

high for her We're out to dare, to do, to

die for her And should de - feat e'er near us

seem Then high - er let our col - ors

stream   And we will   fight   fight   Blue   and

White   fight,   fight   for   Wash - ing   ton   and

1.

Lee   Then   on   for

2.

Lee.

The Fight Song
(Washington State University)

Fight, fight, fight for Wash - ing - ton State! Win the

vic - to - ry_____ Win the day for Crim - son and

Gray! Best in the West, we know you'll all do your best, So

Used by permission of Washington State University

403

on, on, on, on! Fight to the end! Hon - or and glo - ry you must win!_____ So fight, fight, fight for Wash - ing - ton State and Vic - to - ry!_____

Hail, West Virginia
(West Virginia University)

Let's give a rah for West Vir - gin - ia, And let us pledge to her a - new, Oth - ers may like black or crim - son, But for

us its Gold and Blue____ Let all our trou - bles be for -

got - ten, Let col -lege spir - it rule, We'll join and give our loy - al

ef - forts For the good of our old school.____

time boys   to make a   big   noise   no mat - ter what the peo - ple

say_____   For there is   naught to   fear, the   gang's   all   here, So

hail to West Vir - gin - ia   hail._____   It's West Vir -   hail._____

Bingo, Eli Yale
(Yale University)

Bin - go, Bin - go,

Bin - go, Bin - go, Bin - go, That's the lin - go,

E - li is bound to win.

Bull-Dog
(Yale University)

'Way down, 'way down in New Ha - ven town,

Lives Mis - ter Yale, old E - li Yale,

No one ev - er cares to come a - round, Just be -

cause of his pet "bow - wow,"_____

Poor old Har - vard tries it once a year,

Al - ways goes back, tied up in black, For

when Old Yale sicks that big bull - dog on, He

Bull - dog! Bull - dog! Bow, wow, wow,

Our team can nev - er fail,_____ When the

sons of E - li break through the line,

Down the Field
(Yale University)

March, march on down the field, fight - ing for E - li,

Break through the crim - son line, their strength to de - fy;_____ We'll give a long cheer for E - li's men,

We're here to win again.

Har - vard's team can fight to the end, but

Yale will win!___ Rah! rah! rah! win._____ Rah!

Glory for Yale
(Yale University)

win the game to - day, They will learn the same old

les - son in the same old way; Ev - er since we

gave them their first de - feat, Crim - son teams have

fur - nish'd Bull - dog meat, Now it's an - cient

his - t'ry, it's no mys - t'ry, Ask your dad he

knows._____ We've got the en - e - my at

bay,_____ They're in dis - may,_____ It's E - li's   day,_____

They can't re - sist   when   we   at - tack,_____ For there's no

hold - ing Bull - dog   back,_____ Straight for their goal our

war - riors crash,_____ In one long dash,_____ Their lines to

cresc.

smash_____ Blue ban - ners wave the way to glo - ri - ous

tri - umph Yale Will Win!_____

Raise cheer on cheer,_____

Glo - ry is near,_____ Sons

cresc. poco a poco

of old E - li, It's vic - t'ry_____ for

Whoop It Up
(Yale University)

same old sto - ry. The cry is on, on they

come,_____ We'll raise the slo - gan of Yale tri -

um - phant. Smash, Bang, we'll rip poor

Har - vard! Whoop it up for Yale to - day!

ff

day!

fz

Bibliography

In addition to the college and universities whose songs are profiled in this volume, and the OCLC database, the most helpful sources utilized were:

The Allen Official Intercollegiate Song Book: The Foremost College Song Hits, (New York: Winneton Music Corporation, 1962).

Collegiate Song Book, Deluxe ed. (Chicago: M. M. Cole Pub. Co., 1929). (One of several editions under the same or similar title.)

Robert F. O'Brien, *School Songs of America's Colleges and Universities: A Directory,* (New York: Greenwood Press, 1991).

William H. Rehrig, *The Heritage Encyclopedia of Band Music: Composers and Their Music,* Paul E. Bierley (Ed.), (Westerville, Ohio: Integrity Press, 1991-1996).

William E. Studwell and Bruce R. Schueneman, *College Fight Songs: An Annotated Anthology* (Binghamton, NY: The Haworth Press, 1998).

Index of Titles

War Eagle, 3, 6
Washington and Lee Swing, 2, 25, 39
Washington, My Glory, 39
We're Loyal to You, Illinois, 26
When Stanford Begins to Score, 19
Where the Heart Is, 18
Who We Are, 34
Whoop It Up, 41-42, 429-431

Wildcat, 12
Win for Michigan, 28, 292-295
Wisconsin Spirit, 37-38, 383-385

Yale Boola, *xiii, xiv,* 2, 4
Yea, Alabama, 4, 21, 224-226
Yoh Washington, 37, 381-382

Index of Personal Names

Index of Colleges and Universities

Order Your Own Copy of
This Important Book for Your Personal Library!

COLLEGE FIGHT SONGS II
A Supplementary Anthology

_____ in hardbound at $59.95 (ISBN: 0-7890-0920-X)

_____ in softbound at $34.95 (ISBN: 0-7890-0921-8)

COST OF BOOKS_____	☐ **BILL ME LATER:** ($5 service charge will be added) (Bill-me option is good on US/Canada/Mexico orders only; not good to jobbers, wholesalers, or subscription agencies.)
OUTSIDE USA/CANADA/ MEXICO: ADD 20%_____	
POSTAGE & HANDLING_____ _(US: $4.00 for first book & $1.50 for each additional book Outside US: $5.00 for first book & $2.00 for each additional book)_	☐ Check here if billing address is different from shipping address and attach purchase order and billing address information. Signature _____
SUBTOTAL_____	☐ **PAYMENT ENCLOSED: $** _____
IN CANADA: ADD 7% GST_____	☐ **PLEASE CHARGE TO MY CREDIT CARD.**
STATE TAX_____ _(NY, OH & MN residents, please add appropriate local sales tax)_	☐ Visa ☐ MasterCard ☐ AmEx ☐ Discover ☐ Diner's Club ☐ Eurocard ☐ JCB Account # _____
FINAL TOTAL_____ _(If paying in Canadian funds, convert using the current exchange rate. UNESCO coupons welcome.)_	Exp. Date _____ Signature _____

Prices in US dollars and subject to change without notice.

NAME _____

INSTITUTION _____

ADDRESS _____

CITY _____

STATE/ZIP _____

COUNTRY _____ COUNTY (NY residents only) _____

TEL _____ FAX _____

E-MAIL_____

May we use your e-mail address for confirmations and other types of information? ☐ Yes ☐ No
We appreciate receiving your e-mail address and fax number. Haworth would like to e-mail or fax special
discount offers to you, as a preferred customer. **We will never share, rent, or exchange your e-mail
address or fax number.** We regard such actions as an invasion of your privacy.

Order From Your Local Bookstore or Directly From
The Haworth Press, Inc.
10 Alice Street, Binghamton, New York 13904-1580 • USA
TELEPHONE: 1-800-HAWORTH (1-800-429-6784) / Outside US/Canada: (607) 722-5857
FAX: 1-800-895-0582 / Outside US/Canada: (607) 772-6362
E-mail: getinfo@haworthpressinc.com
PLEASE PHOTOCOPY THIS FORM FOR YOUR PERSONAL USE.
www.HaworthPress.com

BOF00